A TALE OF TWO CROFTS

ISBN: 978-1-5272-9522-3

Book design by Suzey Ingold

Cover art by Anne R. Beer

A TALE OF TWO CROFTS

The lives of the children of Acheilidh and Torroble, Sutherland, 1800-2020

Anne R. Beer

Edited by Suzey Ingold

Contents

High in the misty Highlands,

Out by the purple islands,

Brave are the hearts that beat

Beneath Scottish skies.

For Jimmy Mackay of Acheilidh

(1930-2021)

Preface and Acknowledgements

It occurred to me recently that I had never made any great attempt to learn about my grandmother's life while she was alive – this book is an attempt to rectify that. It aims to delve into the fascinating story of a young woman born into a hardworking crofting family who was able to live a very different life from her forebears which, in and of itself, is interesting and inspiring. As an academic, I knew that I had the foundation for a story around the life of this interesting woman and her siblings, as a result of the oral history of the Scottish part of my family locked up in my head for decades.

When COVID-19 began to create restrictions on our way of living in March 2020, I realised there would be an enforced quiet period for me – perhaps, an opportunity to spend the time writing something I had intended to for many years. Now that I was faced with a period without distractions during which I would not be able to go travelling, I decided to give up prevarications and start writing. The result has been this small book based around the life of my Scottish grandmother. She lived to the age of ninety-one. I lived in the same house as her for much of the time from 1941 until she died in 1971.

There are so many other stories connected to Elsie's life that are also worth mentioning and I do so in this book, creating a scrapbook of information about the Torroble and Acheilidh Mackays. It is impossible to recount them all, of course, as they traverse far-flung territory. If the reader can bear with me while I connect the dots, a fascinating picture of a bygone era emerges.

The following story has been put together primarily from oral history, as relayed to me and my siblings by our grandmother and our mother, as well as information offered by extended family members and other connections. I would like to thank my brother, Ian Beer, for his extensive research without which this book would not have been possible and Christina Mackay of New Zealand for her work on the family tree linking Acheilidh and Torroble. I would also like to thank Donald's daughter, Elizabeth, and Brian Robertson and Jimmy Mackay of Acheilidh for their contributions.

Two local history books on Lairg and Rogart were also very helpful. Thanks must be given to the Lairg Local History Society, the Rogart Heritage Society, and the Wick Society. I would also like to thank Emma Crane, for her help with gathering information in the early stages of this project, and

Margaret Crane, for her illustrations. Finally, I would like to thank Judith Vernier for her thorough proofreading.

This work would not have been possible without the internet and I am aware that what is online is not necessarily accurate – I hope any individual finding inaccuracies or who knows of further relevant data will let me know. As I am now rather elderly, turning eighty this year and with slowly failing eyesight, I have been lucky enough in this lockdown period to have been able to work with an editor, Suzey Ingold, who has been helping me make some semblance of sense from the disparate data used in writing this story.

It is very much an expansion of the family history written and published in the 1960s by my great-uncle, William (Bill) Mackay of New Zealand. Bill's history is a fantastically detailed work, done in the days before computerised databases, that involved him traveling the world to locate relatives, which has been the foundation for this new version of our family history. These stories build on the immense amount of work that Bill put into his research. No attempt is made to duplicate his work but rather to concentrate more on what happened to one particular strand of this extended Highland family.

The photographs throughout the book are mostly scanned family copies and, as such, are not of particularly high quality but they do set the scene. A Lochinver photographer, Cathel

MacLeod, also provided several photographs for this book – his wife was a playmate of mine when I was a young child in Lochinver. The spelling of some place names varies depending on the Gaelic or English versions and how it was recorded in history and at present but I have tried to be consistent throughout.

Much information is now inevitably missing and, even with some guesswork, there are still many gaps that I have not been able to fill. All attempts have been made to be accurate in the recording of places, people, dates, and events but, of course, there may be some errors. Responsibility for such errors belongs wholly to the author and editor. If there are any corrections to be made, please get in touch. And, of course – if you have a connection or simply want to say hello, you are very welcome to get in contact.

Should the reader find too much about the environment in the following stories, it is little wonder as, having worked as a town planner on the design of three of the British New Towns, I went on to teach environmental planning for twenty years in the Department of Landscape at the University of Sheffield. I was a Professor and Head of the Department for the last fifteen of those before moving to run my own practice for ten years working for the EU COSTC11 project, examining the potential role of green-structure in cities to enhance environmental quality for those living in them, with the hope of limiting the impact of climate change. Despite being long-since retired, my interest remains in how the environment we each inhabit influences how we live our lives.

Anne R. Beer

Cumbria, England, May 2021

Acheilidh Croft

Torroble Croft

1. INTRODUCTION

The stories here are based on the lives of my relatives, individuals born in the parish of Lairg or adjacent Rogart between 1750 and the present[1]. In particular, it follows the history of several generations living in the Mackay croft in an area of land known as Torroble, which we shall refer to as Torroble croft. These parishes are located in the remote north Highlands of Scotland, an area which has been settled by different peoples for thousands of years.

The whole area is of great interest to archaeologists with evidence of Neolithic settlement (4000-2000 BC) followed

---

[1] See Appendix A: Maps of the Region (Margaret Crane).

by Bronze Age remains (2000-500 BC) and Iron Age remains (500BC-500 AD). Around Lairg lie various standing stones, hill forts, and other ancient monuments. Some interesting Pictish objects, now in museums, have been found over the years in the area, too.

Around 800 AD, the Norsemen settled in the Orkney islands off the north coast of Scotland, their headquarters for trade and raids along the north Scottish coasts. They founded the towns of Wick and Dornoch, as well as many other small settlements along the coast. The entire combined areas of Sutherland and Caithness were held by the Norse Jarl of Orkney, Thorfinn, in the first half of the eleventh century. It is suggested by archaeologists that the name Torroble may derive from old Norse, perhaps indicating that the area was originally a Viking settlement[2]. Upon starting to write these family stories, I had my own DNA tested which came back as 8% Norse, 69% Caithness and Sutherland, with a drop of Irish blood to round it off.

None of us thought of our granny, Elspeth Skinner née Mackay, as remarkable, least of all herself. Brought up, just like her parents and siblings, as crofters in the traditions of Scottish Presbyterianism, she was of the belief that thinking

---

[2] Those interested in a detailed history of the Lairg area should read L. Ketteringham's most informative book, *A History of Lairg*, published by the Lairg Local History Society in 2004. A similar local history has been produced by the Rogart Historical Society.

well of oneself, especially as a woman, was near sinful. She was born at the end of the Victorian period, a time when knowing one's place in society was still very much the way of life. A way of life which, in turn, meant they were expected to behave in a particular way towards those from different levels in society.

In an age where things were moving quickly, yet the divide between social classes remained vast, Elspeth's life is an extraordinary tale of change, industriousness, and adaptation from humble beginnings. That alone does not make her story particularly remarkable – for it was not uncommon to find these traits among Scottish crofters – but what does set it apart is the degree to which Elspeth's life and work occupied a unique role in social and economic change, both for her personally and for society at large.

We begin with a more general overview of crofting life, including an overview of the Sutherland area and its history, before turning to more detailed accounts of the lives of our relatives on Acheilidh and Torroble crofts.

Members of our family lived on Torroble croft from 1870 to 1954[3]. I was fortunate enough to have been put in touch with the last Mackay to live in the old Acheilidh Croft in Rogart, Jimmy Mackay. Over the years, many family members from all over the world called there when they

---

[3] See Appendix B: Earlier Generations of the Torroble Mackays.

returned to Scotland as visitors. The Torroble siblings, including Elsie, were second cousins to Jimmy Mackay. They shared great-grandparents, John and Christina Mackay of Acheilidh[4].

Elsie Mackay   Jimmy Mackay

The stories here aim to explain the demise of the Torroble family croft by the 1960s in contrast with Acheilidh, which continued to function as a working croft until it was sold out of the family in 2005. In 2020, after his wife sadly died, Jimmy took the opportunity to write in detail about his daily life as a crofter over the last seventy years with the help of his daughter, Frances, and son-in-law, Brian Robertson. His

---

[4] See Appendix C: Linking the Acheilidh and Torroble Mackays.

writing very clearly describes the range of work needed to run a croft in Sutherland in recent times, from which the reader can imagine the immense work required to farm the land before power tools and tractors were available. Jimmy recently passed away, in February 2021, at the age of ninety. He is buried at Rogart Free Church.

John Mackay of Balone   Christina and Donald Mackay

The descendants of the Acheilidh Mackays were to spread round the world, like many from other Mackay clan branches, particularly from the 1850s onwards. The stories included here span over two hundred years and three continents, featuring family members who left Scotland to make their homes in nineteenth century New Zealand, as well as across the USA, living at various times in Montana, New York State and City, and North Carolina.

In the story of Torroble, our grandmother, and her siblings, we must start with the parents: Donald and Christina Mackay. Christina was the daughter of Johanna Matheson of Balone, a croft near to Torroble. Johanna married one of the sons of the Acheilidh Mackays of Rogart, John Sutherland Mackay, in 1846. He was a weaver by trade and as such relatively affluent for the time as he had his own business. Producing cloth for clothing, using the old method of a treadle mill, was a good trade to follow as it could generate extra income for the family, particularly in a time before the railway connected Lairg with the cities of the south.

As a child, Elsie knew her Acheilidh great-grandparents well, visiting them with her mother or grandfather in the horse-drawn family trap. When she was there she also used to visit her great-uncle, Alexander – she liked seeing him but also found the poor old chap a bit frightening. He lived in the small building behind Acheilidh Croft all his life, looking after the animals and helping the family.

Johanna Matheson and John Mackay's daughter, Christina, married Donald Mackay, son of boot-

Great-uncle Alexander Mackay of
Acheilidh

maker and mender, Hector Mackay of Dola, and Julia
Grant of Torroble. This union linked two Mackay families:
the Acheilidh Mackays and the Torroble Mackays. Donald
moved to live on Torroble croft after marriage, where they
went on to have twelve surviving children. The siblings grew
up on land Donald inherited from his father.

Elsie was the third born child of Donald and Christina
Mackay of Torroble, Lairg in Sutherland, Scotland. Elsie had

eleven siblings, only one of whom, Donald, was to stay in Lairg for all of his life excluding military service in WWI. Despite what some would consider humble beginnings of a crofting family, Elsie and her siblings came to know personally several interesting and influential people. A handwritten note received from Andrew Carnegie in 1897 would lead Elsie and her brother, Alec, to work directly for the Carnegies and the Bostwicks, the families of two of the richest men in the world at the time. These experiences opened up a world beyond crofting life to them. During the 1900s, while she was in her thirties, Elsie also got to know well the fourth Duke of Sutherland and his wife, Millicent, as well as the fifth Duke after WWI as she and her husband ran one of their properties in Lochinver.

My mother, Jean, grew up in Lochinver and her essay on her life there in the early part of the twentieth century is also included in this work. It vividly portrays life in a particularly beautiful and remote Highland village, surrounded by mountains and next to the sea.

Elsie died in 1971 but her legacy certainly lives on and I believe her story is too interesting not to be recorded. I chose to write this book to keep this history alive, not just for Elsie's family but for anybody interested in the life and times of a nineteenth century crofting community and how the stories of the various people and places unfolded in the following centuries.

To this end, an attempt is also made to trace the stories of family members other than Elsie, including her siblings and their descendants who are now scattered throughout the world, as well as of those of her cousins who remained in Lairg. The story tries to explain something of what happened to those of her forebears directly impacted by the infamous Highland Clearances – although, as a family, their relatives escaped lightly in comparison to those who were cleared off their land and forced to emigrate to unknown territories. The story also brings in information about some cousins who were descended from a Sutherland family who lived on Kinvonvie, another district in Lairg.

I hope to give an idea of the sort of person Elsie was, how she lived her varied life, and indeed what life was like around this time for crofters and those who followed other trajectories, whether out of choice or necessity. I make an attempt to understand how the often harsh characteristics of the life that Elsie was born into, as well as her own early and unique experiences of social interactions in and around Lairg, all influenced the person she was to become. In my memory of living in the same area or house as Elsie for over thirty years, I can testify to the driven, hardworking, and reliable person Elsie was. She was someone always intent on taking care of others and making the best of all situations life was to present her with, including those to thrive on and others that were not always so easy to endure.

Introduction

In particular, my interest here is to relate what we found out about the family to the local social and economic history of the period to create a story of a time now past. One that might, at least, interest the younger generations of far-flung relatives, many of whom now live in New Zealand, with a few in Australia. Very few remain in England or Scotland. From recent contact with a few of them, I also realised the story might be of some interest to various heritage groups in the Highlands of Scotland and New Zealand, as well perhaps to some academics interested in social history relating to people born in the Highlands around 1900.

The stories of Elsie and her siblings are a fascinating insight into life in the late-Victorian and early-Edwardian eras and I hope to do them justice here. The fact that the story is incomplete, as there is a limit to what was recorded by individuals in our family, I hope will not distract the reader.

2. LIFE ON THE CROFT

Croft is the Highland Scottish word for a small – often, very small – landholding rented from a landowner, used to produce food for the family with surpluses for potential sale to raise money to pay the rent.

People born on crofts in those times were far from well-off and normally had to work for a living. All the family members were involved in working in the house or in the fields to keep their family croft going, even as young children. Every croft had to generate enough income from their land by making things which they could sell or by setting up some sort of small business to be able to pay the annual rent. Failure to do so meant eviction. In the Torroble family's case, father Donald eventually set up a carting business in 1879 after the arrival of the railway and the building of Lairg Station adjacent to the land. This business enterprise grew to serve the more remote areas of Sutherland and allowed his children better lives than many but, despite that, they all had to work hard for their family's living.

Nearing the end of the Victorian period (1837-1901) life for rural crofting families was generally a case of hand-to-mouth subsistence and revolved around working the land and feeding one's family. All crofters were required to pay rent to the local landowner. Historically, this would have been clan chiefs but during Elsie's parents' and grandparents' day this was Elizabeth, Duchess of Sutherland, and her husband, Marquess of Stafford.

For crofters, living on their land meant that the threat of eviction was ever-present. There was a certain amount of ruthlessness involved in the business of leasing out land to crofters: one would not want to be in the position of being unable to pay rent. Evictions were common for this reason, with no security of tenure for the crofters and tight margins to operate in. This insecurity underlay one of the most significant periods in Scottish social history in Sutherland and throughout the Highlands – the Clearances – which in Elsie's family case was much less harsh as they were allowed to return to their land once it had been reorganised by the estate. They were luckier than most, having been selected by the

Duke and Duchess of Sutherland to live in the replanned crofting community and thus allowed to remain in Lairg.

Although they were brought up to see Lairg as their home territory, by law only the eldest son could inherit the right to be the leaseholder of a croft, so from childhood there was inevitable social pressure on the other sons and daughters to leave to find work elsewhere as adults. They would need to seek work outside their local area to do well in life – both the girls and the boys of the family alike. In this, they had the advantage of having had the very high standard of schooling available in Lairg School, something most were to make good use of whether they emigrated to other continents or started their own businesses in Britain.

Elsie's parents were to use Torroble croft as a home for their ever-expanding family. All the crofts lie close to one another in Lairg. But for many crofters, acquiring more land was essential to be able to make a living, feed the family, and generally support life. Elsie's family may have taken other land on in the hope of more profitable business and making enough to pay the rent. That they had the croft nearest to the railway was sheer luck, allowing them to run a carting business.

Working the Land

Various published resources have enabled a broader understanding of the often hard life led by those brought up in Torroble. By the time children in crofting families were able to walk they were learning how they were expected to help their parents with food for the family and other, longer-term projects on the croft. In those days of large families, it was expected that they would grow up knowing how to gather foodstuffs together and, in doing so, learn to look after a house or a business. In the Torroble house, there were twelve children to feed, as well as the adults, a family size considered almost normal in Victorian times. All the children were expected to do something to help the family from a very young age, assisting with household or farm chores whenever asked – the girls mainly having to work on household tasks and the boys, once they were older and physically strong enough, helping with the animals and the family carting business.

The croft that Elsie grew up in was, like many, busy and active. Alongside her parents and her many brothers and sisters, Elsie worked every day on the croft to help keep their large family clothed and fed. In those days, of course, there was no state benefit system to help families through difficult times. Without many of the modern conveniences we now take for granted, the thought of keeping a croft afloat and feeding a family of fourteen on top of the day-to-day work is astounding: a massive and never-ending amount of work.

Children finished school at the age of thirteen but, before that, they would normally have helped their parents with daily jobs around the croft – whatever the weather. During this stage of their lives the boys in the family were increasingly expected to help with daily work on the croft, helping their father in the fields and looking after the animals, as well as learning the many making and mending skills a crofter needed to survive off their land. It was essential to learn how to use wood to make and repair fences and gates. To learn how to build walls, as well as repair broken household goods and, in many cases, how to roughly fashion items out of iron. At harvest time, the boys and girls of the family were particularly busy getting the crops in and there were often arguments with the school teachers about the time the children spent away from the classroom.

After finishing school, they all worked on their family croft: the boys learning the skills needed to manage land and crops, and to mend a whole range of farm implements; the girls learning how to look after the house by helping their mother with the whole range of household tasks that were needed to care for a family with so many children.

In addition to helping with the crops, all the children helped with the chickens and cows, particularly the girls. Every croft had chickens which ran around outside the buildings – not infrequently found in the kitchen, too. Often twenty or thirty eggs were collected for the family's own consumption with the surplus sold alongside other produce.

Crofts were also associated with grazing land where sheep, cows, pigs, and goats were kept and where the horses grazed when not in use for ploughing or moving things. However, the horses, looked after by the men of the household, were mainly kept nearer the house, along with the milk cows, looked after by the girls. Horses were needed by any crofter in order to utilise the land effectively in the days before petrol-driven tractors and mechanical diggers existed, available in Sutherland from 1910. Until then, almost everything was hand and muscle work, either by people or animals.

The young lambs that needed hand-feeding were kept there, too. The girls helped with the chickens and lambs, while the boys helped move the large hay bales around and looked after the milk cows and sheep, when necessary.

Elsie and her youngest sister, Kate, always liked keeping chickens and both did so when they ran their own hotels later in life. Looking after the cows was also always very enjoyable for Elsie, although she used to recall a particular story about being chased by one and then being told by her father that an angry cow with a calf was far more dangerous than a bull – a near miss and an important lesson for young Elsie.

Like all crofting families, Elsie's family grew what they ate and aimed for surplus to sell to others for a profit, although that profit generally went straight to the Duke of Sutherland as rent. They grew herbs, as well as vegetables such as turnips, carrots, swedes, leeks, onions, cabbages, and – of course – potatoes. Various legumes and herbs would be gathered and dried in the appropriate season, ready for adding to the pot to make winter meals. Potatoes, the basis of the diet, were grown in the fields, lifted and kept in clamps (covered by earth) until needed for the table. The important thing Elsie always told us was to shelter them totally from the light, otherwise they would not keep for winter use. They were used both for food and for the following year's crops.

Potatoes were perhaps the most invaluable source of sustenance for crofting families in the Highlands: by the 1800s, they were an integral part of every croft and had been for about 200 years. Elsie used to talk of helping her father plant potatoes, and then digging them up and building clamps so that a thick layer of earth covered the potato crop, allowing them to last over winter in complete darkness. She was also taught to look for signs of blight in the crop – indeed, it required constant vigilance for it had life-threatening consequences.

In Elsie's parents' lifetime, after the traumatic events of the Clearances, disaster almost struck again with a period of potato blight in Scotland. From 1846-1856, the blight decimated the main food source of crofting families all over the country. It hit the Highlands in 1846, a year after Ireland, threatening similarly dire consequences due to associated famine. The Highlands were only saved from famine by the British Government being pushed, after much hesitation, by the Highland landowners into a famine relief program modelled on the one put together for Ireland, albeit far too late.

Scotland did not suffer such a poor fate as Ireland, which recorded over one million deaths as a result of their potato famine. The famine relief program also aimed to encourage emigration, by providing free or very cheap passage to other continents. It was fortuitous that these movements of people were happening just at the time the USA was becoming more industrialised and crying out for labour. New Zealand and Australia were also looking for immigrants as farms and businesses expanded. Many hundreds – if not thousands – left on these early assisted passages from Sutherland.

Having experienced the potato blight, Elsie's father ensured she knew what to look out for in the potato crop each year – knowledge that she was to pass onto me when I helped her in the garden. It was a really traumatic experience for Highlanders, unsure initially whether their landowners would help them in any way when the blight hit their main food supply.

Oats, traditionally grown in the Highlands for centuries, were also a key staple grown and stored for longterm consumption. Most crofts had at least one field dedicated to oats and it was almost always a group effort to cut, gather, dry, and store the sheaves when they were ready to be taken to the local miller. It was a time when the scythe was still used to cut the crops and all the boys had to learn to do that from a young age. Even in Scotland in the 1950s, I recall witnessing the crops cut down by the men and gathered into stooks by the women before being carted off.

The Lairg miller would then gather the grains for processing into flour and oats. Some larger crofts did utilise more mechanical methods to process the grain, such as water power or a horse-drawn wheel but, for the most part, it was a matter of human labour alone. Barrels of oats were kept near the house, as well as winter and dried vegetables. Extra stores of oats would be kept in the barns.

As well as providing sustenance to the family in the form of breakfast porridge – weevils and all – dried oats were fed to the animals and indeed this was necessary to keep them going through the winter. Research now suggests that the weevils were actually key to the survival of sailors on long sea voyages as they provided essential protein. The oats reserved for the family's own consumption were generally stored in large wooden barrels somewhere quite warm and dry and scooped out to make porridge on the stove. I remember this from my Granny's kitchen as a child.

Barley, commonly grown on the crofts in Lairg and on the nearby fields, was also the main ingredient in whisky. Although the King's Customs and Excise men did their best to stop the illicit production of whisky, it continued, mostly away from Lairg in the hillier parts of the countryside. Rogart was more successful than Lairg at producing whisky, as it was easier to hide the stills in its surrounding rocky landscape. Whisky production was an essential part of crofting life in the eighteenth century and, to an extent, later, too. When times were tough, sometimes it was only the money secreted away from the sale of contraband whisky that allowed the crofters to pay their rent.

In the days before motor vehicles almost everything eaten was grown near the home and, if not instantly eaten, prepared for winter storage. Without refrigerators and with no grocery shops nearby, one had to be skilled in preserving food for winter months – smoked, salted, and dried. Berries for making jam and nuts for supplementing the diet. Fruit for bottling was picked in the fields and countryside and mushrooms were gathered that could be eaten fresh or kept for the winter.

Sugar was in short supply in remote areas like these but from the eighteenth century sugar loaves could be found in the growing number of local stores. Lairg had a local store in the 1800s, selling a wide range of tools for farming, as well as some materials and condiments by the 1800s. Purchasers bought a hacked off piece of the dark brown sugar and brought that home to use in cooking. A few spices were available, as well as the salt needed to preserve some foods.

Most crofters had a milking cow or two which required milking twice a day – another invaluable source of sustenance. Milk was an important part of the diet and was used not just for drinking and cooking but also to make a local delicacy called crowdie, a type of cheese unique to the Highlands. It was made by mixing rennet into milk to ferment it and then hanging it in a cloth to thicken before squeezing it into its final shape. Most of the world seems to only now be catching on to all the brilliant gut-enhancing effects of untreated fermented milk products like those that were part of Elsie's family's staple diet, and my own as a young child.

There were no pats of butter or cheeses from shops, all those were still made at home until the 1940s. I still remember the making of butter in the Culag from my own childhood. Bowls of milk fresh from the cows were brought to the pantry and left to sit. The cream would be skimmed from the top to make butter and the rest would either be drunk or used to make crowdie.

It is worth noting that none of the milk consumed by Elsie and her family was pasteurised – indeed, it was not the law that it had to be to be pasteurised until at least the 1940s – but this proved generally unproblematic. However, Elsie's daughter, Jean, (my mother) did contract tuberculosis for a short period in the 1930s, most likely the result of unpasteurised milk as a schoolgirl. She luckily recovered fully after treatment in an Edinburgh hospital and wearing a calliper for a year.

Meat came from the family's own cows, sheep, and chickens, which in those days could be slaughtered on the croft as required. Without refrigeration, any meat was generally for immediate consumption or for selling on. All girls were taught how to look after chickens and kill them quickly and efficiently to avoid inflicting unnecessary pain – no chemicals involved, just a flick of the wrist. Pigs would be salted and hung to dry to produce bacon. From my own childhood living in the Navidale Hotel in Helmsdale in the late 1940s, I remember the side of bacon hanging from my grandmother's kitchen ceiling being attacked by Johanna, the cook, with a very sharp knife, chunks being thrown into the constantly bubbling stock pot.

Cows and the chickens were an important component of the food supply. Who looked after the pigs, I do not know, but the swill from the kitchens was probably delivered to them in the yard daily by the women taking it out from the kitchen. That was still done when I was a child in my Granny's kitchen – a great deal of what today goes straight into the bins to be taken to landfill was, back then, fed straight to pigs and recycled as food! No waste left the property. If it could not be disposed of by being recycled, it would be dropped into pits in the fields. Equally, very few poisonous chemicals were ever used and plastic was unknown – even tin cans were quite rare.

Families also often fished the local rivers if they were able to do so without being caught by the landlord's agents who tried to enforce a ban on crofters fishing in streams.

Household Self-sufficiency

With such a large family it was expected that Elsie and her siblings would help with many of the jobs around the croft and this included household chores in addition to tending the land and animals. Like her sisters, Elsie had been taught everything from cleaning the floors and keeping insects at bay to preparing beds and repairing furniture.

It was Christina's job to prepare the girls for adulthood. She made sure all the girls had the necessary skills to run households of their own in the future: ensuring they knew how to clean the inside and the immediate surroundings of the house; how to exterminate vermin; how to bring in water for washing clothes, people, and kitchen utensils; and how to make soups and stews from the produce grown in the adjacent garden. A broth pot was bubbling constantly on the stove so that remnants of food, including animal bones, could be added – just like the traditional French *pot au feu* at the heart of French peasant cooking. This broth could be put into a range of recipes to add flavour.

Most crofting families made their own clothes. It was a woman's job to knit and sew, mainly from sheep's wool, supplemented with what they could buy from the local store. This was another key skill for the girls: making and mending items of clothing for the family which involved spinning the fleece from their sheep to make knitting wool which could then be dyed and knitted into finished garments, particularly thick socks and jumpers – essential for most of the year in the north.

As well as spinning and knitting, the girls all regularly sewed other items of clothing with rolls of cotton. By the 1800s, other materials used for the decoration of clothing could be bought locally. Very occasionally, linen might be available – whether from the local store in Lairg, carted north from Inverness, or reaching Sutherland through local fishing ports, we no longer know. Embroidering clothing likely increased its value considerably. Increasing the sale value of the croft-made clothes would have been considered time well spent.

Sewing and knitting were a major task for the women of these largely self-sufficient crofting families. In the days when there were no clothes shops anywhere nearby, such skills for crofters meant they could make garments for their family, as well as sometimes having something to sell to others. This was one of the few things that women could do to supplement family income on a croft. Elsie spun during her time on the crofts and her spinning wheel remained in our family until it was found riddled with woodworm in the 1960s.

The Torroble girls had the advantage that their grandfather, who lived in nearby Balone, was a weaver like his own father in Acheilidh, Rogart, so they learned much from him about wool and making it into clothes. Elsie's father, Donald, and her grandfather would have also helped supplement the croft income through both his cobblers and weaving businesses. It seems the family even had a shoe shop somewhere in Lairg for a while.

These tasks were something Elsie's mother, Christina, enjoyed later in life, when the family had relatives nearby who helped around the croft. Elsie often spoke of spinning the wool, dyeing it, and knitting clothes for the family.

Tweed was always in demand in the north. It was commonly used for clothing as it was ideal for the weather and was a very durable material[5]. Tweed was woven on a treadle loom at the weaver's home in the colours requested by the buyer. In Lairg and Rogart, tweed was made by our relatives at Acheilidh and Balone. First, the weaver would have wool cleaned as required and then hand-dyed in his range of colours, always using natural dyes so as to produce a range of yarns in various colours. All the work was done by hand, tying the new yarns to the tail-ends of the previous weave which made it easier to thread onto the loom. Using a treadle to weave the cloth by hand remains the sign of good quality cloth.

It is still woven today and produces a very special material. As a child in the 1950s, my school uniform was a dark blue Harris tweed coat – it was the softest and warmest of materials and even good in the rain. As it was still the post-war period, a time of clothing shortages as well as many other things, our school had a second-hand shop so parents could buy and then sell back to the school the uniforms for another child to use. I suspect now that the coat I had at Huyton College in Liverpool was made in the 1930s, before the war,

---

[5] See Appendix D: The Development of Textiles in the U.K. (Jane Mallinson).

and yet it still wore well. The coats made after the war were far less soft so the method of preparation and weaving must have changed. I now know I was stupid not to have kept it – I suspect such a Harris tweed coat would still be warm and weatherproof to this day!

The Mackintosh raincoat, essential for Highland life by the 1900s, was made from a waterproof fabric only invented in 1824. Initially, it was too costly for children but, by 1830, the material was softer and more wearable. By the 1940s, it was commonly used for children's school coats. The material was a rubberised fibre – rubber from Malaysia made it possible to change the lives of crofters who had to spend so much time outside in poor weather. It also improved the lives of fishermen.

Making the family's clothes was an essential skill in all subsistence economies. Even in more well-off families, sewing was seen as an essential accomplishment for all women right up to WWII. Even into the 1950s, sewing was taught to all girls in school – much to my resentment.

The photographs of the time show just how well-dressed the families were in the mid-to-late 1800s. But from photographs of the Torroble family, even from before the railway arrived in Lairg, they look very well turned out – all neatly dressed, sometimes in very elaborate dresses, skirts, tops, and caps. Presumably, they made most of their own clothes and were only able to purchase them if they had any surplus money. Only after 1872 could they travel by train to a town with shops – Inverness was the first place Elsie saw shops but, over the decades, she came to prefer the clothes shops in Edinburgh. I remember going to the shops on Princes Street with her in the late 1940s.

The late eighteenth century travel diary of Thomas Pennant gives a good insight into what it meant to make and purchase clothes in those days:

> In this town [Wick, north of Lairg and Rogart] lives a weever who weeves a shirt, with buttons and button holes entire without any seam, or the lest use of the needle: but it is to be feared that he will scarce find any benefit from his ingenuity, as he cannot afford his labor under five pounds a shirt. (Pennant, 1769, *A Tour in Scotland,* p.195)

Pennant wrote this in the late eighteenth century, around the time of Elsie's great-grandparents' generation, but the fact that clothes were expensive to buy from tradespeople remained true long into the future. It was essential that crofters were skilled in making their own clothes and shoes as, otherwise, although unlikely, they would have needed to make enough profit to purchase them.

With the men of the household out working the land or earning income through their services, most of the household duties were left to the women. It is no surprise that a major part of women's daily lives on a croft, particularly in a family of fourteen, was ensuring that everybody was fed: the cooking and preparation of food was almost constant, an essential skill that Elsie and her siblings learned from an early age as did all children, and one which primed them for later in life.

With all the hard work and expectations of living on a busy croft, Elsie was indeed very well-prepared for her future working in other people's homes and running a substantial hotel business. Another extract from Pennant's diary is telling:

> The tender sex (I blush for the Cathnesians [natives of Caithness]) are the only animals of burden: they turn their patient backs to the dunghills, and receive in their keises, or baskets, as much as their lords and masters think fit to fling in with their pitchforks, and then trudge to the fields in droves of sixty or seventy. The common people are kept here in great servitude, and most of their time is given to their Lairds, an invincible impediment to the prosperity of the county. (Pennant, 1769, p.202)

Although this was written some hundred years before Elsie's birth, it is a familiar story among women in places like rural Caithness and Sutherland. Work did not stop when they married but simply took on a different form, still with the requirement to satisfy the landowner's demands for the rent.

It is worth remembering that daylight hours are very short in the far north during the winter period so the women must have struggled to work on their weaving and spinning with only the light produced by oil lamps and from the fire in the hearth.

Another income stream for a family were the goods made on the croft: fashioning wood into special shapes to act as tools or crafting farm implements from metal.

Itinerant tinkers – small family groups who, for centuries, wandered the north with their horse-drawn carts and tarpaulin shelters to repair and mend household and farm items – came regularly to each Highland village and to many scattered crofts and other dwellings, besides. Even in the 1940s, when I was a child, they were still around. I remember my grandmother shouting out in excitement from the car, "there are the tinkers!" as we drove through the Assynt area, near where the Duke of Westminster had one of his homes at the time.

From Highland records, it appears the tinkers liked the Westminsters best of all their clients as they were so well fed there. Unfortunately, other records of the 1950s show members of my family, the Skinners of Overscaig in Lairg, had difficulties with the same tinkers. In those days, before modern communications, grievances were often long-lasting.

It is difficult now to comprehend what rural life was like in the 1860s when Elsie's parents were working on the crofts. There were no local shops stocked with ready prepared food, no electricity to light the house at night, and no piped water. Indeed there were also very few leisure opportunities for the children of the croft, there being so much work to do and no electricity or modern means of entertainment. Before electricity, there were only oil lamps and candles, and water was usually pumped by hand from the nearest well and taken to the house in tin buckets. Bowls and jugs of water commonly sat on tables to enable family members to wash, with any luck using water that had first been heated on the stove. This system for ablutions was still in use in very remote areas without piped water even as late as the 1940s.

When the siblings lived in Lairg, their drinking water came from a well and was disposed of on the land. A burn (stream) ran near the house, providing water for animals as well as cleaning the house.

Clean drinking water was a problem for all in the past. This was made more difficult by the fact that animal excrement, as well as human waste, used to be piped not far from the buildings on any croft to be used as fertiliser on the fields. It must have been a constant source of potential infection, although by no means as bad as it was in Victorian cities at the time, where it would have been an ever-present danger.

Laundering clothes involved large tin buckets with carbolic soap to soak garments in before using scrubbing boards to remove dirt, again ideally using water that had been heated on the stove or a fireplace. Then, if the croft possessed a wringer, putting it through that or leaving it to drip-dry. After all that, the clothes and sheets were ironed with the iron heated on the kitchen stove. With a family of fourteen living in the house, this was a mammoth task undertaken – needless to say – by the women.

There was no laundry in Lairg until 1928 but it was possible to pay women from other families to come as domestic servants to the croft to help with this major task and other household work. In Elsie's family croft, it was only when some of the children had left home that Christina sometimes employed domestic servants to help with the immense task of doing the chores and keeping the croft going.

Before the arrival of the railway in Lairg and Rogart in the 1870s brought coal, the main source of heat would have been peat fires. The stone fireplaces in each croft were often designed to have small ovens on each side for bread and stews and, by the 1800s, it was also common to have an iron grid on top on which to boil pans of water and cook other foods.

Some wood would have been available for the fires but not much – there was little woodland left as the majority of the Caledonian forest had been felled and exported by sea to England during the eighteenth century to drive the Industrial Revolution. No profit from that sale went to Scotland as a whole, just to the landowners. The sale of the great Caledonian forests was a way for clan chiefs to make money as they met the demand for timber to feed new industries and the rapidly growing cities resulting from the Industrial Revolution. This exploitation of the forest meant there was little wood left for crofters to use.

Peat was an excellent alternative source of energy for fires and was a way to make good use of locally available materials. To transform it into a useable material, peat was first cut from the ground in small blocks, then laid out to dry outdoors where it had been cut. Once dry, it was transported – most commonly in large wicker baskets, but also sometimes in a horse-drawn cart – to the place it was stored for winter. The process involved the whole family and we see evidence all over Scotland of the continued use of peat in a very similar way. Especially in remote villages, cutting the peat as a communal activity continued for some time after WWII as it was a cheap source of fuel.

I remember in the late 1940s being taken by my grandmother into old crofts in Lochinver when she visited women, some of whom had worked for her in the pre-war years as staff in her hotel. My memory of these visits is still the overpowering smell of the burning peat: a thick smell which permeated everything including clothes, especially the men's, as in those days many crofters and fishermen wore thick tweed jackets and trousers that were almost never washed as it would have made them less effective when working outdoors in the rain.

Indeed, peat-cutting was such a long-held tradition in Scotland that there would have had to have been a very compelling reason for it to be replaced by coal. Of course, as things changed in Lairg and Rogart, so too in Lochinver, and today we see a different picture. Peat is still used, albeit usually as a fertiliser rather than as a primary fuel source, as electricity is available everywhere.

Although oil and coal became available in rural Scotland first via sea routes, crofters were rarely able to afford these more expensive fuels. In the pre-railway era, unless one lived near a port it was near-impossible to access these resources, anyway. Around forty-five miles from Lairg, a steamship arrived weekly in Lochinver, travelling up from Glasgow bringing food, coal, and other supplies to west coast towns and landing them all at Culag Pier. Closer to home, supplies landed at the newly-built productive port of Helmsdale, giving access to goods being transported along the east coast. A small seam of coal had also been mined at Brora, about twenty miles east of Lairg, but this, too, was not available for most crofting communities.

With a lack of expendable income, combined with the difficulty and expense of transportation, it was simply not feasible for crofting families like Elsie's to even consider a shift to coal-based energy – at least not yet. Once the railway station in Lairg became operational, Elsie's father set up as a coal merchant for the area and that business was profitable until Elsie's brother, John, sold it.

The arrival of the railway in 1874 was to change life significantly in Lairg, including the ability to access resources like coal. However, familiar barriers to modernity still remained among crofting communities and it is no surprise that peat continued to be the main source of fuel for families like Elsie's for decades – well into the twentieth century.

When the Sutherland Estate sold their rights to the land within Lairg in the 1920s, the new landlord, philanthropist Sir Edgar Horne, did many things to improve the quality of life in the village, including installing a generator in 1928 which brought electricity to the crofts for the first time. However, a village-wide electricity system did not arrive until the 1940s. Sir Horne also built and ran a laundry. These changes instantly made a great difference to the women in particular.

Just think about living in the early twentieth century with no light other than smelly candles and oil lamps, and no piped water until its arrival in Lairg in the mid 1920s. By 1954 there was a proper water supply, pumped by the power generated by the hydroelectric scheme that used Loch Shin to generate power for most of Sutherland.

Education and Finding Work

In her Sutherland crofting roots, Elsie clearly had a deep sense of home and belonging, but the effects of education were to change the course of her life. Elsie may have been brought up on a croft, but she was well-read and well-educated thanks to both the ambitions of her parents and the outstanding Scottish public education system. From 1696, every parish in Scotland had a school and schoolteacher and the Education Act of 1872 made schooling compulsory for both girls and boys from the ages of five to thirteen. In 1888, new regulatory standards were introduced for secondary schooling and, in 1890, school fees were abolished completely.

Various Scottish governments over the centuries seem to have recognised the political and economic importance of having a nation of well-educated children and, by the early

1900s, the Scottish system was very egalitarian, to the extent that children from all strata in society were taught in what was, objectively, a very accessible and high-quality system. Generally speaking, there appears to have been a much higher standard of education in Scotland than in England for centuries, not just for the elite but for the mass population.

Indeed, the quality of education in the local school which Elsie and her siblings would have attended in Lairg must have been very good if one goes by the skilled, economically successful lives that they led. By all accounts, the school provided both boys and girls with a very thorough grounding in a wide variety of subjects. Such rural schools were generally overseen by the local Ministers of Religion and this seems to have helped ensure high standards, since the Ministers were often the only people with a university education in remote areas.

Unfortunately, it was during this time of her life that Elsie developed a rather intense dislike of the local Ministers, whom she remembered as being overly concerned about religious adherence and what one could *not* do, rather than truly stretching children's minds and encouraging critical thinking. This irked Elsie greatly because she said it made Sundays so boring – the children were supposed to do nothing but read the Bible, walk outside quietly, and behave themselves. She particularly lamented being told off for reading the wrong sorts of books on the Sabbath.

Though the quality of education was objectively very good, Elsie's memories suggest for some children perhaps a rather stultifying experience. Elsie actively resisted any attempt to control what she did in her spare time. Elsie was anti-church all her life as a result, and my mother was brought up as an agnostic – something, funnily enough, my father only discovered after he had married her, himself a very strong believer who had even thought to become a Church of England vicar before the war!

Aside from this, not much is known about Elsie's time at school. What we do know, however, is that she had ambitions for her future and they necessitated a good command of English. Like her siblings, Elsie was a Gaelic speaker until she finished school at the age of thirteen when she came to the realisation that if she wanted to be anything other than a crofter's wife, it was imperative to have good English in addition to – or perhaps even entirely replacing – Gaelic.

In part, this was due to the Education Act of 1872, decreeing that English was to be the only language used in schools. As such, by the time she finished school, Elsie was already more or less fluent. Through their teachers, many children came to see Gaelic as the language of a backward people while English was understood as the language of the future. Speaking it well was necessary if one was to obtain better-paid employment opportunities and so, on her final day of school, Elsie decided never to speak Gaelic again except with her immediate family. To this resolve she remained true, as did her siblings.

Looking at my Mackay relatives, it seems to me now these children of relatively uneducated crofters were a very bright lot. They were born into a time when they could become relatively well-educated so there was the possibility that if they, as individuals, chose the right skills to learn and develop, they could easily manage to have interesting lives.

Elsie and her daughter, Jean, were both very bright, as was John Ronaldson Skinner, Elsie's husband. He himself had gone to school in Golspie Academy and Wick Academy where he was Dux (top boy) of the Academy in his final year at school in 1894.

The education system in the nineteenth century was, however, certainly skewed in favour of boys and the opportunities for them were significant. That said, it was still unusual for boys from crofting families to go on to further education. University education had been available for centuries in Scotland – far ahead of the English system – but was mainly designed for the children of the land-owning classes. Boys whose parents could afford to put them through the fee-paying school system were generally expected to move into the university system, some at the young age of thirteen. For some, the church was another way into higher education.

Consider James Matheson (1796-1878) as an interesting case study: he was the eldest of the boys of the Shinness Matheson family of Lairg, who were not relatives of Elsie's family but who, in the mid-nineteenth century, were Lairg's wealthiest family (aside, perhaps, from the Duke of Sutherland's family) and lived not far from Torroble. James was taught at the local school in Lairg then went on to the Royal High School in Inverness for a year or so before moving to the University of Edinburgh.

He studied to become a surgeon just so that, despite his young age, he could travel as a doctor aboard an East Indiaman on its journeys around the ports of the East India Trading Company. On arrival in China and Hong Kong, being involved in the notorious opium wars, James went on to become one of the two founders of the trading firm Jardine Matheson which was at the time the biggest business on the London stock market. James's money was initially made through opium trade and then, with his firm's wider involvement in Far East and Indian trade, in tea and other goods. By 1841, the company had nineteen clipper ships – the fastest sea transport of their day – and they owned hundreds of small cargo ships.

When he returned to London, he was awarded a knighthood and was very well-respected, not to mention one of the wealthiest people in Britain. For a time he was also an MP. Later, he bought the Isle of Lewis and spent large sums of money in an attempt to improve the quality of life for those who lived and worked there. James married but had no children. After his death, his estate, including both Shinness and the Isle of Lewis, passed to his nephews and then (either in part or in full) to the industrialist, Lord Leverhulme.

It was James Matheson's education at a Lairg school which initially enabled him to become such a successful entrepreneur, despite being born into a family living in such a remote part of Scotland before widespread transport links.

Under Scotland's traditional crofting system, there was no guarantee that children, other than the eldest son, would have land of their own to use once the official tenant died. Even in a settlement like Lairg, if local populations grew too fast people had to leave to seek work to survive. From the eighteenth to nineteenth centuries, a time of generally large family sizes in the post-Clearance period, the need to find employment elsewhere inevitably grew for those for whom there was no work locally.

It was not uncommon to find families as large as Elsie's with her eleven siblings, all of whom would need to find their own way in the world. There was an inevitability about the movement of people from areas with insufficient employment possibilities to support the forming of new families. In fact, it was this, along with legal changes to land ownership forcing many crofters off their land, which provided much of the surplus labour needed for the British Industrial Revolution and, later, the growth of those countries which are now ex-British colonies. By Victorian times, when children's survival rates began to rise, large to very large families became more common and, thus, the exodus of people from crofting communities like Lairg increased.

Indeed, most of Elsie's siblings ended up leaving Lairg as the crofting system was not able to support a good life for a large family nor provide employment for these relatively well-educated people. Many of the boys left as they could see no future in Lairg as, other than the eldest son, John, they were landless and so forced to look elsewhere for employment if they wanted to form families of their own.

This had been a longstanding issue in Scotland as schools and universities trained many young adults who, from around the seventeenth century onwards, found that they had to move to England or to the colonies if they were to obtain employment suited to their skills. For young women in rural Scotland, the opportunities were more limited, being generally confined to marriage, crofting, and work in other households.

Daily Life in a Changing World

In the absence of cheap and easy transport, walking was the way most people got around in Elsie's day. Notwithstanding the fact that life was essentially self-contained in a crofting community – mostly out of necessity rather than choice – everything that was not grown or made locally on the croft's land could only arrive by horse and cart or be carried in on people's backs. There were many places crofters needed access to that required a long walk on foot, including school. The man who was to become Elsie's husband, John Skinner, had an eight mile walk to school each day in the late 1890s.

The roads were mostly in an appalling condition throughout Sutherland until the 1900s. There were no county councils in those days so the local landlords were responsible for the roads. It was only when the fourth Duke took over the Sutherland Estate that measures were taken to improve the road system using estate funds. Given that Sutherland was a very extensive area, it is easy to understand just how bad roads sometimes were, well before tarmac. The estate ordered the crofters on their land to give a certain amount of service every year for the upkeep of roads and repair of bridges. As the area was remote, there was little pressure to improve the roads until the end of the Victorian period when the rich started travelling to the north – just because Queen Victoria used to make extended visits to Balmoral Castle once the railway system began to reach the north of Scotland.

The state of the roads in Assynt (1910s)

Like all more well-off crofters on the reorganised model farms, father Donald had a horse and cart which the family used to get around the village, to collect the wool which was prepared mostly by the wives of local crofters and their daughters, as well as to deliver ready-made lengths of tweed to individuals to turn into items of clothing.

The Torroble croft, like others constructed by the Sutherland Estate at that time, had initially been designed to have extensive grazing land – in Torroble's case, to the south. When father Donald first took over the land from the landlord, it was likely this grazing land still existed. However, the building of the railway through the croft's potential grazing land, leading to the opening of Lairg Station in 1874, left this area much reduced.

The railway system was put in by the Duke of Sutherland, initially to move coal which was found on the east coast near Brora around the county and, in particular, to bring it to the parts of Sutherland lacking fuel, to stimulate industry. Petrol-powered engines came later and were adopted by the Mackay family around 1900 with Robert being trained in the maintenance and use of powered vehicles. From before the railway in Torroble was built, Christina's father, John, was involved in meeting the trains at Rogart and delivering goods to and from that station, the first in the area, including the cloth that needed to be taken to customers.

The advent of the railway station in Lairg changed many things about life in the area. The railway can never have made great economic sense, being part of a link from Inverness to the far north of Scotland where few people lived. More likely, it was initially a strategic move made by the Duke of Sutherland to carry goods to and from his lands and to encourage visitors. In doing so, the railway opened up access to the rest of the world for typically very poor crofting families.

Prior to the arrival of the railway and then buses, Sutherland crofters were still, for the most part, living in what we might now term a pre-industrial economy. Once it arrived, local families were able to access goods that were previously unavailable to them. Food stuffs, household materials, and tools could now be purchased easily, and the lack of disposable income to buy such goods was becoming less of a problem now that crofters could easily transport and sell handmade goods and surplus food to the south or the coast. The seeds of a modern capitalist system were sown and the exchange of goods and money became increasingly commonplace. With the arrival of goods also came the arrival of people: the number of visitors to the Highlands increased significantly from the 1860s onwards, aided initially by public knowledge of Queen Victoria's love of her holiday home at Balmoral.

The railway also brought news, in the literal sense, with the daily arrival of newspapers and their stories of what was happening in the rest of Britain and the world. This, combined with the compulsory teaching of English in all Scottish schools, ensured that those in the remote Highlands were better connected to and aware of the outside world than ever before. It is no surprise that one inevitable effect of this development was learning of new employment opportunities elsewhere in Britain and overseas, and this contributed to the emigration of a significant portion of Lairg and Rogart's local population in the latter half of the nineteenth century. The railway and the education system together thus transformed the nature of life in remote Scotland, and Elsie's family were right in the thick of it.

The loss of land in monetary terms for the Torroble Mackays, which might have adversely influenced the income needed each year to pay the landlord, was more than compensated for by the possibility of the family setting up a carting business, one to take goods to and from Lairg Station. It eventually grew into a substantial business using the family's horses and carts, supplemented once the motor age arrived from the early 1900s by small, petrol-driven vehicles.

Elsie considered herself lucky because she grew up with her family's horse and cart haulage business. The crofters were free to run other businesses – the only provision being that the croft's rent was paid in full each year. Our family also used this system to their benefit in both Acheilidh and Balone, running successful weaving businesses. In the 1860s, her mother's parents, John and Johanna Mackay, who lived nearby in Balone just north of Torroble, also used a cart to get around and take his cloth to purchasers.

Elsie's father, Donald, started his carting business in the 1870s. He improved and expanded it with the arrival of the Bonar Bridge to Golspie railway linking to the station at Lairg. The family's carting business mainly meant picking up people, as well as goods, and moving them to both local and distant locations. Weekly, the carts would go as far west as Lochinver, north to Tongue, and east to Dornoch. At one stage, they seem to have had a delivery contract with the Post Office and packages were brought to the family croft daily for onward delivery.

Over many years the business was successful enough to substantially enhance the family income beyond the bare minimum needed to support themselves – an entrepreneurial vision that changed their lives. Eventually, father Donald made a real success of the carting business. By 1900, he was thinking about the use of lorries for moving material.

The carting business was a financial godsend for the Torroble family. It appears the family was involved in the carting of goods until the time his eldest son, John, returned from America following Donald's death in 1932. The work was too much physically for John and he sold the coal-merchant part of the business. That, in fact, was probably a sensible move. With new modes of transport becoming more common, the demand for coal dwindling, and electricity arriving, there was less need for their services.

The family cart would travel all over northern Scotland bringing goods from Inverness and southern Scotland and taking goods to the places the railway system never reached. Initially, father Donald made these longer journeys but for some years after his father's death, young Donald continued to offer a carting service across Sutherland. It made the family better off than many others living on the same sized plots of crofting land. Granny and her siblings had a slightly more affluent life than many of their generation living on the new farm areas. Not all were so fortunate to be able to grow a business.

The Torroble Mackay family carting business used to serve the whole area of Lairg and, ultimately, as far as the settlements north of Lairg and on the northwest coast. My grandmother, Elsie, and her niece, Elizabeth, both talked about the very special trips they made – albeit, generations apart, Elsie in the 1890s and Elizabeth in the 1950s. Their fathers drove the carts, stopping at many small places for the night as they criss-crossed Sutherland.

Keeping a family alive on a croft was hard work for children, as well as adults, and Torroble croft was no exception. The Torroble family coped well as can be seen by the fact that of her fourteen babies, Christina only lost two babies at birth or near after. The twelve remaining siblings survived and thrived and were able to lead very active lives in several different countries – USA, Canada, New Zealand, and England, as well as Scotland. They were not damaged by the relatively harsh environment in which they grew up. They were strivers, who were all to do well in their very different ways. That they were all fit and able enough to leave the croft to live and work far from Lairg suggests that the lack of clean piped water in their early years must have been a problem their family solved.

As for Torroble croft, once most of the boys were gone, money was needed to hire other labour so the necessary work could be done. Sometimes other local women were hired in to help Christina with household matters as can be seen in the Census of 1881 when two servants were living in the house. It was not just Torroble which experienced manpower problems in these times – other crofts, too, had to hire in women to help do the household jobs. These problems were only exacerbated with Christina's death in 1920.

Torroble Croft (c.1905)

3. A BRIEF HISTORY OF SUTHERLAND

Sutherland covers a large part of the far north of Scotland, featuring some of the country's best and most dramatic scenery. Lairg is located in northern Scotland about eighty kilometres north of Inverness. There are few settlements nearby, the nearest of any size being Golspie on the east coast. The surrounding landscape is hilly and wild, like much of the Highlands, with some astoundingly beautiful landscapes. It sits next to Loch Shin from where the River Shin flows to the North Sea at Brora, passing through the Kyle of Sutherland and Bonar Bridge.

For hundreds of years, the area around Lairg appears to have consistently attracted settlers despite its generally poor soils and harsh climate which, combined with its relatively remote geography, makes it feel like somewhat of a hidden gem to visitors. There were long periods of time when this part of Scotland was fought over by various invaders from Europe and the south. The local people have a reputation as fierce warriors, a characteristic still evident in modern life, particularly in the twentieth century with so many young people from the surrounding areas dying fighting during the two world wars.

The main clans populating the area historically have been the Mathesons, Sutherlands, Murrays, and Mackays, along with their propensity for violent battles – although today they are much more amicable! In general, the clans are no longer as important as they once were although they still retain a presence. Since the seventeenth century, the clan chief of the Mackays has been titled Lord Reay and this family lineage, together with that of the Duke of Sutherland's, linked the Mackays of Sutherland and Caithness – a large part of northern Scotland. At present, the fifteenth Lord Reay, Aeneas Simon Mackay, is clan chief.

While at one time Lairg was a small crofting community, today it has a population of around 800 people and benefits from summer tourism to support its population, with many of the former crofts having been converted into holiday accommodation.

The nearby settlement of Rogart is smaller with a present-day population of around 450 people. Rogart was where Elsie's grandfather lived as a weaver, hence the connection between Elsie and her siblings and the Acheilidh croft in Rogart. The Parish of Rogart, as it exists today, was probably established in the first half of the thirteenth century when Alexander II created the first Earl of Sutherland. The church that presently stands in the centre of Rogart, which dates back to 1770, is likely the latest version of many.

The Sutherlands had the biggest area of township land in Lairg in the early 1800s. Townships were small clusters of related families, living in close proximity in small crofts. These are not towns in the modern sense but rather units of land. Each township could well have had specially skilled inhabitants, such as cobblerss, weavers, and perhaps even a tailor. From sixteenth century documents, Lairg is shown as being composed of eleven townships, including Kinvonvie and Torroble with the church in Wester Lairg. Dola and Craggie are also names mentioned, not as townships but as local names for units of land.

Torroble, where Elsie's family croft was situated, was one of several groupings of crofts in Lairg resulting from the reallocation of land by the Sutherlands in the early 1800s during the period known as the Clearances. Elsie's family would have inhabited the croft from then until 1954. The group of crofts on Torroble – as well as communities in

Balone, Kinvonvie, Milnclaren, and Tomich – were, in effect, part of a New Model Farm scheme, the likes of which had been imposed on parts of agricultural England from the seventeenth century and had led to large increases in productivity and profitability. This resulted in many having to leave these areas as there was insufficient land for each existing tenant to stay.

The Sutherlands

Elizabeth Sutherland (1765-1839) was a Scot, who inherited the earldom of Sutherland at the age of twenty upon her father's death as there was no male heir. Elizabeth's family had held the earldom of Sutherland since the year 1230 and could thus claim to have been landowners of much of the northeast and northwest of Scotland for centuries. Their forebears had acquired the land by being clan chiefs in earlier generations.

She married an Englishman, George Granville Leveson-Gower (1758-1833), an exceptionally wealthy industrialist. He ran his estates in England and she ran her land in Sutherland, albeit with the help of English land managers (factors) appointed by the Duke to help her. The pair were a force to be reckoned with.

The Leveson-Gower family was one of the wealthiest families in Britain in the eighteenth and nineteenth centuries, prospering massively in the Industrial Revolution through involvement in canal building and the various new chemical industries, amongst other things. However, by the beginning of the twentieth century, things were changing for them, due mainly to the large inheritance taxes they had to pay on the death of each head of the family. Nevertheless, the consummation of the Duchess's power and control through marriage to George ensured that they retained ultimate control over most of Sutherland and its people. By 1816, they owned 63% of the county of Sutherland.

The Sutherlands began to take an interest in the economic potential of the area at the end of the eighteenth century. Much of the family's income in Scotland was generated by the annual rent paid to them by their tenant farmers – the crofters. Many of these were almost destitute, frequently only just scraping together a living for their families from small plots of land in areas of poor soil associated with frequent failure of crops, due to diseases such as the potato blight (1846-56). Failure to pay the annual rent frequently resulted in eviction and that, in turn, reflected badly on the Sutherlands. So, being established industrialists from England, they looked for more profitable uses of their assets.

After their union, the clearances began in north and west Scotland. As unjust as it seems to us now, the Sutherland estate and their land managers were just following the practice of reallocation of land, which happened over many decades in Scotland – even earlier in much of England. The couple were well acquainted with the ideas of King George III – commonly known as Farmer George for his interest in improving agriculture in England – who encouraged the introduction of various farming practices applied to increase productivity and modelled on various schemes introduced in his native country of Germany.

The Assynt area, within which Lochinver is the largest settlement, was one of the areas subjected to the infamous clearances from the late eighteenth into the nineteenth century. These resulted in a massive reduction in the number of people living in certain parts of the Scottish Highlands and considerable ill-feeling among those who lost their homes. The area of farmable land was significantly reduced, its main use being for hunting and even that only allowed by permission of the Dukes of Sutherland. Those evicted were driven like cattle from what they had held, by clan tradition, as their family's land for centuries. Many west coast crofter and fisher families quit the Lochinver area and emigrated to

New Zealand, Australia, Nova Scotia in Canada, or the USA at this time[6].

Around the same time the Sutherland Estate was 'improving' Torroble, it also initiated schemes to remodel the areas of Lairg including Kinvonvie, where cousins of our family lived, and Tomich. This remodelling was most likely the reason why Donald Mackay was appointed the leaseholder of the Torroble croft by the Sutherland Estate.

Reallocation of land was particularly common in the Midlands, where the new Duke's forebears had prospered. In England, this period of history resulted in many English peasant farmers losing their right to farm and being driven from what they understood to be their own farms. It was a time when many had to leave the countryside to seek work so as to support their families. They moved to the newly built industrial settlements growing all over England as new industries boomed: the improvement of the roads; the introduction of the canals; and, later, the rapid construction of a railway system that made raw materials more quickly available to new factories and processed goods to markets. This same process had an impact on southern

---

[6] See *Watchman Against the World – The Remarkable Journey of Norman McLeod and His People* by Flora McPherson, the excellent book on Norman McLeod, the local church minister born in the eighteenth century who led his people to the other side of the world from Assynt.

Scotland, too, initially contributing in particular to the growth of both Glasgow and Edinburgh from the late eighteenth century.

George succeeded his father as Marquess of Stafford in 1803 and was given the title Duke of Sutherland upon his death in 1833 by King George III. Elizabeth died in 1839.

Their eldest son, also named George Granville (1786-1861), became the second Duke of Sutherland. In 1823, he married Lady Harriet Elizabeth Georgiana Howard. Their son became the third Duke, George Granville William (1828-1892) who married Anne Hay-Mackenzie (1829-1888) in 1849. Their son Cromartie (1851-1913) became the fourth Duke of Sutherland, his Duchess the Lady Millicent St Clair-Erskine (1867-1955) whom he married in 1884. Although Millicent outlived her husband, the title of Duke passed to their son, George Granville (1888-1963) upon his death in 1913.

Millicent, Duchess of Sutherland

A signed photograph given to Elsie around 1913 for her work with the Culag Hotel

The Clearances and New Model Farms

The Clansmen of the Sutherland Estate, who were members of the Mackay Clan, were driven off their land starting in 1807, many moved off by the estate's factors with the help of soldiers. In that area of Lairg, very large numbers lost their homes and means of livelihood. Many lost their lives but most eventually emigrated from Britain, often under a very elementary form of an assisted passage scheme, set up by the landlords and the government to rid themselves of the problem.

In 1811, the Sutherland Estate decided to remove all their sitting tenants from Torroble, Kinvonvie, Tomich, Milnclaren, and Lower Lairg. Torroble was the last of the districts in Lairg redesigned by the estate so as to make farming more efficient and, thus, increase productivity and the rent they could collect from their crofters. Creating these remodelled areas was, in effect, a part of what is known as the Clearances (1750-1860).

However, the areas of Kinvonvie, Tomich, and Torroble were subject to a very different treatment compared to the majority of crofters living on Sutherland-owned land, in particular the land to the north of Lairg which was turned into a vast sheep farm. Our family were fortunate to be allowed to return to what had been their home territory after the reorganisation. It is not known quite how the reorganisation was carried out – it is likely that the Torroble men had to do much of the work themselves. Records from the Sutherland Estate might give more clues as to this.

The intention was to rehouse some of the sitting tenants but not all. At present it is not possible to ascertain the proportion allowed to return to live and work as tenants on land that had been, in their minds, theirs for many centuries. The estate's aim in the reorganisation was to rearrange the land into "neat little farms to suit industrious tenants" as William Young, the estate factor (land manager) wrote in his letter to the Duchess in 1811. The objective was to remodel Torroble and other areas of land into more profitable units to make more income for the estate.

All this was done on the direct instruction of the Duchess. She was using ideas from her husband's experiences of the Agricultural Revolution in the English Midlands. There, his family had already improved productivity on the farmland land within their estates. As the Marquess of Stafford, he was very involved in the Industrial Revolution, too, well used to reorganising estates and towns to make them more efficient and profitable for him as it increased the revenues to his estate from industrial and open farmland. All of this would have been good news for the economy and for the wealthy landowners who could profit from such actions but led to terrible conditions of life for those unable to find work. In some areas, whole families were homeless; in others, leaving countryside homes was a slower process, allowing time for families to adapt.

His Scottish wife, Duchess of Sutherland, was persuaded that such ideas could equally apply in Scotland. What might happen to the individuals thrown off their land does not seem to have been cause for concern.

The reasons for the Clearances were many but the underlying factor was that there were too many people for the area of land. The land in Sutherland was mostly of too poor a quality for successful agriculture – put simply, not enough food could be grown to support the constantly expanding population of the nineteenth century. The aim of applying this reallocation of land process to Lairg was to make farming of crofting land more efficient. At the same time, the estate paid to build better quality homes for which they could charge rent.

The agricultural revolution enabled England to escape this problem by increasing the productivity of the land. However, the soils in the north of Scotland were not understood; nor was the fact that the weather conditions of the much harsher climate in the far north of Britain meant that farmland was naturally far less fertile. As such, the same level of productivity could not be met – the differences in quantity and quality of productivity does not appear to have been understood in England at government level either.

Prior to the clearances, a drift of Highlanders leaving the poor land their forebears had subsisted on began after the 1745 rebellion, with substantial numbers of crofters taking their families overseas to Canada, the USA, Australia, and New Zealand from the north of the Highlands – all well before the Clearances. Those who left at this time tended to be the more active and efficient crofters, ambitious to find new homes where their families could prosper.

For the Sutherland Estate this was a problem, as it was the very crofters who were most able to pay the annual rent who chose to leave. Those who emigrated before 1800 tended to leave behind the less ambitious – the clansmen who were later to be moved to make room for sheep. Many of these men could not find the sums needed to pay the annual rent and it was these people who were eventually driven off the land by the estate factors when it was decided to turn their land over to supposedly more profitable grazing sheep.

The families who were moved, many of whom were physically driven off their land, had nowhere to go. They were first pushed up to Strathnaver and then to the coast where the estate had the idea that they could feed themselves by fishing and growing crops on small areas of land, with the possibility of harvesting kelp from the sea. This would give them something to sell to the estate in return for cash which could be used to buy seeds for planting. The Duke of Sutherland came from a family that made much of its money in providing chemicals for the Industrial Revolution and the iodine from kelp was in high demand.

Once they had moved to the coast, many found passage in sailing ships to other countries – made possible by subsidised passages on sailing boats, paid for in part by local Sutherland landlords and government schemes. Many also moved south to the areas of growing industries that were hungry for labour. Many are thought to have died before finding other employment. The Clearances remain an event inducing much bitterness, even today, but the events of the period were much more complex than is often realised. The land the clansmen worked for centuries was too poor to support the numbers living on it. The tragedy was that another way of solving the problem was not found.

The grandparents and great-grandparents of the siblings would have been affected by the reallocation of land undertaken by the Sutherland Estate during the Clearances. They were not amongst those thrown off the land their family had worked for generations but were instead allowed to stay or, in some cases, moved to other locations within the Lairg area. These were typically sites where the estate had reorganised the crofts and built new dwellings for the crofters. Allocating each family a certain amount of land to support daily life by having sufficient land to grow their own food to feed their family was a characteristic move of the period. For example, my great-grandmother had twelve children so there was intended to be enough land for ample food and a surplus to sell so as to be able to pay the annual rent.

The Torroble area was remodelled into a Model Farming Unit in the mid 1800s along with Kinvonvie and Tomich, two other crofting areas in Lairg. Experts on Model Villages were persuaded to come north to advise on how the layout could be improved. In many ways, the advisors replicated what had been done with similar projects in England in the eighteenth century not fully understanding the different soils and climate of the Lairg area. These areas were reorganised by clearing the land in each, then laying out the houses, barns, and farmable land more efficiently in terms of potential productivity.

Hector Mackay and Julia Grant, father Donald's parents, were there during the reallocation and were the first to live on the reorganised Torroble land. As the first to live there, they would have had a new house and attached barns for the animals, as well as a good water supply from the adjacent stream. They would also have had land for growing crops, both to feed the family and, with any luck, generate sufficient surplus to sell to raise money towards the annual rent. There was also access to other land for grazing. This was how Donald inevitably inherited the right to the Torroble land.

A croft in Sutherland

Around the time the Torroble land was finally cleared by the Duchess in the 1800s, our family members probably considered themselves fortunate to have been allocated a good-sized croft in the New Model Farm scheme. The land managers were tasked with being very careful about who got the new tenancies. Given the relatively small size of the new farm units, they needed tenants with the skills to pursue other money-making activities besides just being crofters.

Donald Mackay had the necessary skills to make and mend boots and shoes and thus supplement the croft's income. When his children were young, there was mention of him running a small cobblers business in Lairg whilst working the Torroble croft so as to raise sufficient funds to pay the annual rent.

It also turned out they had been very fortunate to have been allocated that particular croft since its land was right next to the new Lairg Railway Station when it was constructed in 1896. Once this was up and running, it enabled the family to set up their carting business which was an important source of income for them.

At the time, the estate rebuilt all the buildings on the Torroble land using pattern books thus creating a standard design. Each of the new model crofts consisted of a main building and a garden for growing food. The family lived in the main house. Nearby buildings were used for the storage of food supplies, both for the family and for animals, and, beyond that, open land for grazing. The main house of that type still standing is Balone, a good example of the most common design chosen by the Duchess of Sutherland.

Nearby Balone was where the Torroble siblings' grandparents, Johanna Matheson and John Mackay lived. The estate's factors implemented the schemes, working directly for Elizabeth, Duchess of Sutherland. Despite her affluent husband, it was primarily Elizabeth who organised the redistribution of land that was at the core of the mass movement of people during the Clearances.

The Torroble house was larger than many others built at that time and was a slightly different design from that of Balone. Unfortunately, it is no longer standing. I stayed there in the late 1950s and remember a substantial house with chickens in the yard and views of the adjacent countryside. It had to house a family of fourteen as well as, not infrequently, hired labour. It fell into disuse after the last tenant, John's, death.

It is interesting to think that by the early 1800s, people were living in what were essentially planned settlements, perhaps even the first housing estates. Even more interesting that such settlements were built in what was the relative backwater of places like Lairg which at the time did not even have a sufficient population to have a recognisable town centre.

Having spent thirty years living with a grandmother whose family memory retained the inequities of the Clearances for all Highlanders, it has been interesting to realise that there was more than one kind of story to come as a result of the Clearances. For the hundreds of thousands of Highlanders that left Scotland and found themselves in new countries and lands with a great range of opportunities to enhance their lives, the Clearances can almost be seen as a blessing. For my forebears, the changes during the time of the Clearances did present the opportunity for a better life in the 1850s and 1860s, the first generation after the Clearances. For those who stayed in Lairg, there was the improved land allocated directly to them by the Sutherland factors, while the following generation had the possibility of emigrating so that they were able to live much more economically successful lives than their own parents and grandparents.

However, this did not stop my grandmother, Elsie, being full of wrath about what happened to so many of their kinsmen living in the Lairg area from 1814 to 1819. Granny remained uneasy about what had happened all her life. There is no doubt that Elsie and her siblings would have met the children of the dispersed Highlanders at school, those who somehow managed to stay living locally. In those circumstances, Granny found herself met with hostility and learned to be very angry about what the Clearances had done to other people in the Lairg area.

As children, she often took us to Strathnaver and told us the history of the people who had lost their land and the terrible way they had been treated, with many dying. Although I was only five years old at the time, I will always remember these visits because of her sheer and abiding anger.

The Kinvonvie Boys

Meanwhile, the leaseholder of Kinvonvie, John Sutherland, who held an area of farmland containing twenty-seven crofts, realised that the proposed remodelling of the Kinvonvie land as the Duchess envisaged could only result in totally inadequate parcels of land for his sons and relatives. John and his wife, Janet, had four sons – George, William, Joseph, and Robert – all of whom, in his opinion, needed land. Then, there was also the problem of the other cousins, including several cousins of the Torroble Mackays who needed to be housed and fed. The proposed remodelling would not just be a problem for his family, but for any future families in the area who would have insufficient land from which to make a living with the estate factors having allocated only two acres of land per family.

John also recognised that only his eldest son, George, would inherit the right to work his part of Kinvonvie. Around 1835, George left for Australia at the encouragement of his father, soon followed by his other brothers. This was at a time when there was a mass of individuals wanting to leave for Australia from both Scotland and England, so there were many boats to choose from. John gave each son a substantial sum of money to start their new lives.

According to records, George arrived in Hobart by 1836. Joseph arrived in Hobart in November 1835 via Calcutta, where it appears he spent some time buying goods to trade in Australia. Robert also made his way to Hobart. For a time, all the boys appear to have settled in the Port Philip area, near where the city of Melbourne grew. They are also known to have bought land in the present city centre of Melbourne, as well as buying the rights to sheep runs near Geelong.

The Kinvonvie boys in Australia seemed quickly to have turned into profitable businessmen, buying and selling the right to use land to raise sheep. As this was Crown land, the land could not be owned but the rights to its use could be sold. Both Robert and Joseph signed a request to buy land at Port Philip which was where most goods from Van Dieman's land went. They lived at a station on Sutherlands Creek – named after them and still known as that today.

Robert also applied for a license to use land south of Port Philip. By 1838, he had over 3,000 sheep. In 1839, he purchased a plot of land in what was to become the city of Geelong. In 1840, he licensed 22,000 acres called Native Creek which he held until 1864. He licensed another 122,660 acres in Rich Avon which he held until 1857 and another run called Konongwootong which he held until 1870.

Joseph bought lots in Port Philip on Flinders Street and just off Queen Street. He was involved with setting up the

Bank of Melbourne and the Melbourne Gentlemen's Club House.

Not much more is known about George other than that he died in 1859. There is little record of William although one Lairg record shows that he died in 1862. It appears that George, William, and Joseph all died in Australia of various illnesses and left their holdings to their remaining sibling, Robert. There is an estate named Kinvonvie near Melbourne but it is unknown whether it relates to the Kinvonvie boys. The current owner says the land was purchased by Irish forebears long ago.

Robert returned to Britain around 1860, building himself an elegant, Georgian-style house in Egham, north of London. In modern terms, Robert Sutherland, who was brought up and schooled in Lairg, was probably a millionaire when he returned to Britain. He seems, however, to have had an antipathy for Lairg, perhaps feeling his family had been ill-treated by the Sutherland estate.

Although he did have female servants come down from Lairg to look after his house and occasionally saw some relatives, for the most part he seems to have avoided much contact with Lairg and apparently never visited. There is mention of other cousins from Lairg living in London when he was there and that he was in contact with them.

He also built a smaller house near his home for his nephew, Joseph Macdonald, and Joseph's wife, Annie, who looked after Robert as he aged. Like Robert, Joseph had been in Australia and likely New Zealand, too, involved in financing railways and coal mining projects. It was he and his wife, Annie, to whom both Sutherland House in Egham and their home, Lairg House, were left. Both houses were later sold to generate cash for Robert and Joseph's cousins, as well as the many charities Robert supported.

These two houses in Egham were on land that is now the grounds of Royal Holloway University, an all-women college until 1900 when it became a constituent of the University of London. The newest building at the university is called Sutherland House.

Robert bought himself a coach and horses and had a coachman to drive him round town or to show visiting relatives around London. He is said to have been a collector of paintings and to have moved in high society. From his own resources and the inheritance from his brothers, it is clear he had sufficient funds to present himself in Victorian society as a gentleman of leisure.

As a gentleman about town, he eventually became a member of the Royal Geographical Society. He had apparently been corresponding with them while in Australia, sending information on what we would now term environmental issues. As a geographer by training myself, with a speciality in environmental planning, this link with a distant cousin has amused me.

None of the brothers who went to Australia married. When Robert died, he left large sums to charities in the north. He also left substantial sums to many cousins in Lairg, leaving some distant relatives very well off. Some of these cousins were related through marriage to the Torroble family. He was a very wealthy man and very generous, also in death.

However, the majority of Robert's money trickled down through Joseph Macdonald and his children. This money was eventually used to buy the Dola and Craggie estate in Lairg and to build Sydney House – a stylish gentleman's residence and one of the largest houses in Lairg.

Sydney House was built by James Mackay – the son of Hector Mackay and Julia Grant, the husband of of Annie Macdonald, and the father of Hector and Joseph. James had emigrated from Lairg to Australia and, after building up some money through various jobs, decided to buy some land in Sydney, adjacent to the sea – only to find, after a few years, that it was where the city's fathers had decided to construct Sydney Harbour as more berths were needed for shipping. So, James, who like the other Mackays had a crofting background, arrived back to Lairg a very rich man and turned himself into a gentleman by buying the land and building

Sydney House. It was probably his experiences in Sydney that gave the house its name. Sydney House is still in use today but, unfortunately, is no longer in the family.

Sydney House

James's son, and one of the cousins of the Torroble family, Hector Mackay eventually inherited the house. Hector – who we all knew as Hector Sydney – was someone all the Torroble siblings and their families knew well. He was on good terms with the Torroble siblings and other cousins, particularly in the post-WWII period, inviting them regularly to meet in his house and to use his garden and estate. There were many other cousins who stayed in the Lairg area who went regularly to his house for tea and a chat, looked after by his housekeeper, Mrs Elphinstone. In particular, Mrs Elphinstone was a source of all family information for Elsie post-WWII.

The Dola and Craggie estates were used up to the mid-twentieth century for hunting, shooting, and fishing by local gentry – mainly friends of Hector's. My grandmother and her siblings were invited to regular meetings at Sydney House whenever they returned to Lairg from their homes in New Zealand, Canada, USA, southern Scotland, and England. We remember Hector's great kindness with the help of Mrs Elphinstone in hosting parties for his extended family in his house and garden, sometimes allowing those interested in fishing to have a day on Loch Craggie, renowned for the quality of its fishing.

On one of our last visits to see Hector, I'm afraid my father disgraced himself entirely and came back to Sydney House with nothing. Really, my mother, Jean, should have been the one to go fishing, as she had been taught the art by the gillies as a child living in Lochinver. She learned to fish at Inverkirkaig, still one of the best stretches of fishing in north Scotland today.

It turns out, through our great-great grandmother Julia we are linked to Hector Mackay – he is our first cousin twice removed. In the 1930s, my mother was taken twice on winter sports holidays to Switzerland. Mother learned to skate, while Hector and his friend and cousin, Hector Ross, who ran the Sutherland Arms Hotel near Dornoch by the golf club for years, enjoyed their annual holiday of curling on the ice in a mountain resort. Mother enjoyed those holidays immensely, especially as she could practise speaking French. It may have been that experience which persuaded her to go to the hotel school in Lausanne after school as part of her training to help run her parents' hotel. The two Hectors were helpful to many of our family. Aside from Jean's winter holidays, Hector Ross also found a job for Donald's daughter, Chris, in the hotel.

After Hector died, his estate went to his nephew, Graham, and the regular visits ceased. If the internet is to be believed, Graham married twice. Like many of the well-off of that time, he was said to enjoy playing cards for high stakes with the local gentry. But he was unlucky: in the period between him taking the estate over and when he died, it had to be sold. He moved in different social circumstances and was, unfortunately, involved in big investment schemes which failed such as the building of the new Scottish skiing resorts in the 1950s and 1960s. When he died, his daughter, Josephine, had to sell everything including, eventually, Sydney House. Unfortunately, we have been unable to trace what happened to Josephine. One of Graham's wives, a Finnish woman named Inger, is buried in Lairg cemetery.

Hector Ross

Hector Ross in Dornoch.
Donald's daughter, Chris, is in
the front row, second on the
right.

A family gathering at Sydney House

Top: Mrs Elphinstone, Kate, Chris, Hanna, Tommy, Helen
Bottom: Hector Sydney, Elsie, unknown, Alec

It was a sad end to our Torroble cousins' link with Sydney House which is now used by holiday-makers. Much of the Dola and Craggie land was eventually used for forestry. Dola is left unused but Loch Craggie is sometimes still used for fly-fishing. All the siblings and their children, now in their seventies themselves, still remember meeting in Sydney House, particularly in the 1950s and 1960s.

Several houses in Lairg were built by cousins of Hector Mackay over the years, some with money passed down from the successes of Robert and his brothers in Australia. These include Balcharn, Bridge House, and New James Villa.

4. THE ACHEILIDH MACKAYS

James Murdo Munro Mackay was the last Mackay to live in the old Acheilidh Croft in Rogart who finally quit crofting in 2005 and moved away from the area in 2010. He died in February 2021. This account details his daily life as a crofter over seventy years. It was written with the help of his daughter, Frances, and son-in-law, Brian Robertson.

I suppose it lands on me to tell the story of the last Mackay family to live on the crofts at Acheilidh, Rogart. I was born in Rogart and my great-uncle, Alexander Mackay – or Sands, as he was called locally – was the last to live in the cottage known as the Acheilidh Mackay home. More recently, my father and I used that house as a tool store holding a mass of equipment and tools for all occasions. It even had large peat knives and spades, a work bench, and all a man-shed should have. One noticeable thing about the building was that over all those years it was dry inside. It was one of the driest buildings in the area despite being on the hill in the Strath, taking the full force of the western winds from Lairg.

Acheilidh from Muie, looking southwest

If it had not been for the change in the land structure, the crofts at Acheilidh could have been much damper as the changes made in previous centuries had held back the tidal river Strathfleet and made Rogart less tidal. That meant the tidal water previously got to Rogart near the mart. The only giveaway of the previous land condition is the flat basin of good fertile soil noticeable as you drive east through Rogart to the Mound on the east side of Sutherland near Golspie.

There has been much said and asked about the meaning or translation of the name Acheilidh. Recently we checked the best translation and consulted a local expert who, using the Gaelic and local pronunciation, confirmed the best as:

Ach-Choillidh   Wood-field

That could well be the answer as the field in front of the house and along from Granny's has a group of trees in the middle. They have been there for many, many years, as opposed to the fir trees near Rowan Cottage.

Some say the name was originally French-Scots and when the maps were produced in later days the writers, because it was the Highlands, tried to make all the names Gaelic, be it right or wrong. So, we could look at a map of the area and all the locals would not recognise the places as they were written in Gaelic. We can blame the cartographers for that. Most names in the area, if not all, are Gaelic or Norse.

Acheilidh, as I knew it, was several crofts with three houses: Sands's, Granny's (Burnside Cottage), and Rowan Cottage. After Sands's brother, Angus Mackay (b.1835), and my father, William, I lived in Rowan Cottage with my wife, Anne, and our family after carrying out renovations and extending the floor space to accommodate the family. The house sat proud on the hill facing north, the area reasonably flat which accommodated the double garage I put up for the car, quad and the like, a hen 'hoose' and room for a static caravan and turning circle. A small plantation of firs planted in the fifties served as some sort of wind block from the west and the dog kennels hid behind this group of trees. This area made for a pleasant lay-by area off the single-track road that came up from the railway heading along past the Sutherland's house towards the Munro's at the top of the road which rolls back down to the railway and the main route to Lairg and Golspie.

The Acheilidh Mackay Family Tree

My father was William Mackay (1887-1975) who married Ruth Munro. William's father was Murdo Mackay (1837-1893) who married Lena Munro. Known locally as Big Murdo, my grandfather was a weaver in Rogart. Murdo was also Sands's brother, both children of John Mackay (1794-1875) and Christina Sutherland. It is amazing that in a few generations there are so many people related to the Mackays. Many a time, we or my sister, Annie, who lived in

Golspie, have entertained family descendants who have come back to their roots. Over the years we have seen people from New Zealand, Australia, and Canada with various surnames as well as Mackay.

Acheilidh, looking towards Granny's

My father, William was a gamekeeper at the Rovie estate with Joyce Rawstrone. Her father was Major Priestley, head-keeper; Dad was the under-keeper. The Major had several staff, chauffeurs, servants, gardeners, and keepers. He was in

85

business with Lancashire lace-making and gained a portion of the company when a shareholder died. William worked in the gardens. At some point, with the cutbacks, he was washing the dishes and the Major was drying them! William was awarded a Gallant and Distinguished medal as a soldier in the Seaforth Highlanders in the First World War.

William Mackay's war effort recognition

William's brother, Angus (1878-1939) was a Committee man and involved with crofting and the administration of the local crofters. He was a regular visitor to Edinburgh on business. He was planning to marry a girl from Edinburgh. Unfortunately, he had a brain tumour. It might have been possible for him to survive if action had been taken earlier. Unfortunately, it had developed so much that it was not possible to remove the tumour and he died at the age of sixty-one.

Both the brothers were good at carpentry although Angus was the better of the two. Angus would make barrows and carts and was the one who was going to upgrade the house at Rowan Cottage. He had all the items from timber to cement but with his health issue, he never got the house improvements started.

There are two graveyards in Rogart with Mackays buried in the old and new yards. There are other Mackays not so closely related to the Acheilidh Mackays also in these yards. John Mackay (1794-1857) is in the old yard. My father, William, is in the new yard.

I was brought up in Burnside Cottage – what, in later years, we called Granny's house – with my parents and Annie, my older sister. After school and spending time working the land with my father, I worked for a time away from home. I had a spell with the Forestry Commission and, when work was plentiful in the west due to the hydroelectric work being carried out, I joined the squads to get the job done. Staying away from home in Overscaig, I met my wife to be, Georgina Anne Corbett – known as Anne[7]. We married in the 1950s and set up home in Blarich Cottages and then Rowan Cottage.

Jimmy

Anne

We had two children: Christopher, a gifted carpenter, and Frances, an office worker who later excelled in care. In fact, she looked after Anne and me for five years after we left the croft in 2010. My son died in a car crash in 1972. All my hopes for him and the croft were dashed in one blow. I never

---

[7] Born 1927 in Kinlochbervie, died 2020 in Perth.

really got over it. But Anne and I carried on with the great loss. Frances was still at home at that stage and she was most helpful in the work of the croft.

Frances and Brian

Before retiring, I ran the croft with sheep, some cereals for feed, a few cattle, and some chickens. I supplemented the crofting with work on the local railway. I walked the line for a period and then was working as Station Master at Rogart. I had a share in the common grazing giving access to further grazing for the sheep on the hill behind the croft.

The landlords have changed over the years. Crofts are owned by the landlords and the croft is rented to the crofters under certain conditions. Previous generations have expected more from the landlord and, because they work the land, the crofters feel a special attachment to the land.

With absentee landlords it is understandable that communication can be distorted. The crofters in Assynt were able to buy their estate from the selling landlord back in December 1992. This was a worldwide news item where the underdog won! I found the story encouraging and thought it might bring a new impetus to the crofting lifestyle. There are several Scottish laws to safeguard this way of life. It is monitored by the Crofters Commission.

For some time, my landlord was Sir John, a fine gentleman, not afraid to do a bit of heather-burning himself. He was always friendly and businesslike. He was an extraordinary man. I do not know where he got his energy from, a man in his eighties and as fit as someone a lot younger. He was reluctant to ask others for help but would call on his wife.

Upon my retirement, the croft was sold to Donald and June Ross. They built a new house and continued the croft in a similar manner. Anne and I lived in our house, Rowan Cottage, 'onsite'. After some fifty years in Rowan Cottage, Anne and I moved to live with our daughter and her husband in Perth in 2010. Both Anne and I moved into a care home in Perth but, sadly, Anne died in July 2020.

Rogart Life

My recollections of life in Rogart are mixed. There were hard days and good days, but it was a really challenging lifestyle. One needs to temper the romantic view of your own place where the days are long and sunny and there are no cares in the world. It was far from that with animals to feed, vets to call out, jobs to do, and, because of where we were, quite long journeys to get basic supplies. There have been numerous books showing a somewhat romantic view of crofting life which is far from the reality of the lifestyle of many. Daily chores like mucking out the byre must be carried out no matter the weather! It kept me fit, though. The hill from Sands's house to ours is steep and I tried to walk it a minimum number of times a day!

The cycle of crofting from the highs of lambing, lamb sales, and spring-summer days bringing in the peats certainly compensated for the winter days of wind and blasting rain. In later years, snow was less of a feature but we have had severe winters where we were cut off for days in the white-out of blizzards. The winters of 1954, 1968, and 1981 are memorable. Dark nights with no streetlights meant looking out of a window to oblivion and a distant glimmer from the nearest croft some distance away.

The smell of the hay as it is turned for drying and storage for the winter was a great encouragement to us, even though it was a back-breaking job. Then again, in our climate, we were turning several times as the rain or morning dew ruined the previous days efforts. To get the hay in was a task completed and a sigh of relief. Most years the equipment worked well, be it tractor, rakes, or baler. The in-house thresher was situated in the steading opposite Sands's house. It was a musical machine like a vast clock where we dropped in the corn sheaves at the top and out came the corn and residue with chaff.

Many a time I had help from a friend, Bobby Scotson. He was a retired man, originally from Glasgow, who loved the croft and lifestyle. He had a place in Oldshoremore and would visit us at job time or when the car needed a MOT. I can still remember Bobby, Frances, Anne, and Brian lifting potatoes, rows and rows of potatoes, from the sloping field in front of our house east of Sands's.

Yet over the years at peak times of business or when real problems needed help, the local neighbours would stop what they were doing and come and give a hand. Likewise, when you looked across the Strath you could see when others needed a hand. As people retired and moved away, this activity became less. I know there was a lot more working cooperatively in Father's time.

My nearest neighbour for many years was Andrew Sutherland, a Presbyterian, a man of faith and a brilliant negotiator. He worked a smaller croft to the east of Acheilidh with his wife, a teacher, and their daughter. Like me, Andrew worked to supplement the croft, in his case with the county. Between the crofts was a stream which flowed down the border of the crofts under the railway on to the Strathfleet river near the Mill.

Ian Mackenzie was a quiet Highlander who lived across the Strath at Muie. He had an additional croft on our side and my lasting memory of Kin, as we knew him, is him sitting in the car in the lay-by at the top of the road, considering life, and gazing across the Strath in the direction of his house. I really do not know what he was thinking about but he did a lot of it.

Down nearer Granny's house, the small three-bedroomed cottage near a second stream, was a bridge over the water to John MacLeod's. He lived in a croft that his parents had. Originally, he lived with them in Muie. He could still see his parents' house with a stretch of the neck. In his later working days, he ran a bus company to support the locals. The school contracts I am sure helped greatly. He presented the Psalms at the local Free Church of Scotland, where I was a member and a Deacon. He moved on to retire to Muir of Ord.

As you come back round from the garages and John MacLeod's there is a hill back to my house, a single-track tarmac road lay in front. To the left was a red corrugated shed. A small shed that I used during lambing, putting ewe and lamb together to help in the mothering. Hector's house, as it was known, was a very old building. Hector's has a twelve-foot square floor with timber supports and low walls of stone with the corrugated roof now coming apart but the shell is still solid.

I do not know much about Hector. He was a shepherd, probably working for Blarich farm. He never married. Hector Leslie died in 1937 at the age of ninety-four, when I was still just a child. Most probably, he was the son of William (1815-1895) and Mary (1813-1877) Leslie of Tulachbuie, Rogart. Mother said he was a lovely, gracious man – a devout Christian. When he needed a drink from one of the brooks he would take his cap off as a sign of thanksgiving. I was in Hector's house after the funeral and what amazed me was there were dozens and dozens of empty whisky bottles, all different coloured glass. I could not understand why he had kept all this glass.

Beyond the croft fields to the common grazing is the hill heading south towards Bonar Bridge. A mass expanse of volcanic rock covered in heather and grass for as far as the eye can see. One place on route that we called the Greens was where, at some point, the ground had been cleared for grazing and it may have been a summer grazing spot. There is still a load of large stones – I think there might have been a house there at some time. This area was a good walk from the ends of the crofts and passed the apportionment, an area taken out of the hill and added to the croft. The apportionment was a large field used for the sheep. It was steep in bits with a stream flowing down the east side and a stone 'stell' enclosure, handy for sheep protection in a gully, ideal for a picnic – but never did have one! At the furthest point it looked onto the waterfall which is marked on maps.

The Greens still produced lush grass and was a stop-off point for a rest whether walking or taking the quad bike to the furthest areas of the hill. Near this spot was where we would dig the peats and stack them for drying, lifting, and gathering on the cart to bring back after the summer weeks. Stacking them in the shed near the house was followed by the relief that it was done for another season. To know we had fuel for the fire and those dark wintry days was gratifying.

The peat days were a family highlight. We would set off, tractor, trailer, tools, and dog with family and picnic up the hill past the hill park, winding up the hill on the track to the plateau of the Greens and onto the next section where the start of the peat banks stretched out towards the southwest and Torroble. The summer months of drier weather and the smell of the fresh grass was a great comfort to us as the heat of the day brought our temperature up.

Lunch was a good time to cool down from the beating sun with the slight wisp of wind to cool the body. Of course, there were the midges, those horrible insects that tickle and annoy you to extreme! At the end of the working day the trip back down the hill was the cool down as we saw our little settlement, with the sun on our backs lighting the roofs, as they came into view and then the walls, garden and the caravan sitting proud to the east.

Everyone needed horses in those days. Most or some would have two horses. Willan Mackenzie, along the road, had two horses. Jackie Macleod's mother had a horse in Acheilidh – they moved to Muie later.

Sandy Murray, William's neighbour, had two horses. William kept the horse for him. You needed two horses for work, especially ploughing. This was a good arrangement. One horse, Bulon, was a lovely mare. One night I was taking her back in to the stable. I jumped on to the horse and we headed to the stables. I then realised that the stable door was open, and we were heading straight for it! As we got to the door entrance I was expecting to get a rather hard knock on the head from the lintel, but the mare stopped right at the doorway and I got down off the horse. It was reassuring that the animal had anticipated the situation. Fraser had a horse as well. It could come along the road, and often did, for a bit of grass.

A winter's day outside Granny's, looking towards Hector's

At the back of Granny's garage was a long dry store that took my tractor and equipment, and a fenced funnel I used for moving the animals. At lamb sales we would gather the sheep for sale and funnel them around the back of the garage and up to a raised gated platform the height of the animal float, which could reverse straight to the gate for easy boarding. I always felt it saved a lot of time – a slick operation. If you have ever tried to move animals you will know what I mean! Anything to make life easier is most helpful.

Then, of course, over the years my assistants to the animal movement were the dogs. A real asset on the croft. When you go to the hill to gather sheep or simply to check them, a dog is so important. I have had several dogs over the years all with different characteristics. Corry, Moss, Ben, and Jeff were their names. My last dog, Jeff, was a little timid but was a good worker. I am sure I could have got more out of him with more training.

In between the big jobs, I carried out various improvements to the crofts. As well as the house extension and the garage down near Hector's house, fencing was an ongoing job and I set up water to the house from a spring up in the hill. It served us well over the years although some summers there was little to no water flow. With various television aerial installations, I tried to get the best picture from a weak signal. The new Rayburn was great for the hot water and the heating in the kitchen, the hub of the house. At some point we moved to the oil-fired Stanley which was cleaner but meant the need for the peat was reduced.

I put up the garage at Rowan Cottage and extended it to hold a car, quad and a work bench together with all the garden tools and lawnmowers – yes, lawnmowers plural! New gates and tracks helped for efficiency and the garden beds near the house were used mostly for vegetables. I grew rhubarb down the field from the trees and, in the latter years, I cultivated a vegetable plot in the field above the railway on the lower ground near Granny's.

For the bulk of the season, the sheep were in the hill – that is, the common grazing south and in the high land north of Bonar Bridge and heading to Strath Tollaidh. It is a good day's walk there and back to gather sheep. Up past the Greens and due south along the fence bordering two different estates and past the two lochs, as we called them. Maps call them Loch na Saobhaidhe and Lochan na Gaoithe along west of the large hill known as Meall Meadhonach. These are Gaelic names, as mentioned in maps, and I do not think our forefathers called them these names.

One time, I went to gather sheep with Brian, Frances's husband. They were living in Invergordon and sometimes came up to help especially at lambing time. We got to the Meall and had our lunch sitting on the Meall looking south east to Strath Tollaidh. A hillside faced us, not steep but flowing and green with grass where my sheep sometimes headed. It was the remains of a settlement never used in my lifetime but the improvements in the land were still evident in this green area. One can make out the outline of the settlement of houses and a broch at the top of an incline.

We sat for a while talking about things and recovering from our walk. A warm day and a slight breeze all added to a pleasant seat with a terrific outlook. It was evident that there were sheep at both sides of this large hill. I took the dog and headed north on the east flank. Brian went back the west flank past the lochs and along the fence to pick up those on that side. It was well into the day when I returned to the croft. It was even later that a tired-out son-in-law returned with a few sheep. He had walked back and forward to bring in the sheep travelling miles to get one. Sheep are difficult to handle: if it is too fast, then they scatter; too slow, and they will just go off in tangents. The lesson here is – have a dog when gathering sheep. The sheep dog trait is to go wide around everything. They have a gathering instinct.

Gathering the sheep could have been for one of several reasons – dipping, clipping, or lamb sales. Other trips to the hill could be for burning heather. Left to its own, heather grows strong and coarse, almost bushy. This results in less grass growing which is not good for the sheep. Trimming back the heather and gorse (yellow broom) by burning in the early part of the year was a task that everybody knew had to be done but no one really wanted to carry out. If memory serves me right burning dates have changed over the years but are allowed up until the end of March. The problem being that at that time the ground is still too wet.

Never go burning on your own or by two. Three minimum to carry out the task. There needs to be beaters to stop the flanks burning out of control. It is a fine line between getting a good fire and just little patches of scorched growth. The grass comes through again no problem. The wind is the thing to watch. You do not want a neighbouring estate coming after you because the fire has travelled and burned the fencing! My aim would be to carry out an area every year. But as the years went on less use of the hill meant those using the common grazing were less and the need for burning was reduced.

Muie burning (2010)

One day my landlord, Sir John, and I, went early to the hill to carry out some burning. Unfortunately, things got out of hand and of the fires, three or four got away, taking off on all sides. The fire brigade was called for and they came and sat at the bridge near the gates to the hill. They never bothered going up. Thankfully, the fire petered out because it was a very calm night with an air of frost. It did get to the fencing and it was an anxious time for me. It is a very dangerous game doing heather burning!

Another time of local involvement was the dipping, a practice now stopped for health reasons. Gathering the sheep, and as a team, getting all the sheep through the 'fank' along past Andrew's and back again was a full day's job. There were moments of time to pass and talk of local events or news. Today, other methods are used to protect the animals for various ailments and creatures.

Another full-on time over a few days was the clipping. I still preferred the hand shears and have spent many an hour, back aching, clipping the fleeces for the wool marketing board and seeing the price year on year fall to virtually nothing. I had a few pens and a concrete base at the back of the sheds ideal for the clipping or marking and in full view of the sun. Most of these jobs were dependent on the weather. I needed to read the signs in the sky to decide on whether to carry out the job or not.

The tups (male sheep) were released to the ewes around October for a spring lambing, a bit later than the national average to benefit from slightly warmer weather. Tups would be hired in normally from the northwest as I felt they produced a hardier animal. With the addition of feed supplements, all I could do was wait.

Ewe and twins at lambing

So, in the weeks from mid-April to the end of May it was all hands on deck. One lamb would come then another and at the height of lambing it could be double figures per day. I held the pregnant ewes in a large field that had been taken out of the hill. This field was relatively near the house which made the checking trips easier. Of course, on the last check at night I would find that the ewes had gone to the furthest end of the field up near the waterfall for peace and quiet, giving me a longer walk out and back!

Most years were good, and we had a few sets of twins and the odd crippled or deformed lamb. At birth I would take the ewe and lamb into the croft fields for a check-over, giving the mother a feed for strength. Mothering odd lambs meant bottles of milk on a regular basis. As the days moved on my strength would improve, then at the end of the lambing tiredness would be back.

All these days Anne would be helping too. She was feeding the chickens, keeping house, keeping the adopted lambs at the fire feeding with bottles, and there was forever a washing line hanging outside the garage on the flat grass above the house. There always seemed to be good drying days.

By the end of May, we would have bookings for the caravan and some of the holiday folks we got to know through repeat bookings. Indeed, some enjoyed mucking in with our work as part of their holiday. By this time, it was the final checking of lambs and marking them for the future.

Usually around the May Bank Holiday weekend, subject to warm dry weather, we would gather the sheep and lambs over a few hours into batches putting them through the pens and check them, count them, and work out how many male or female lambs there were. After attending to the tasks, we rejoined all the sheep and let them settle for the evening making sure that as could be seen all lambs were with their mothers. Marking the lambs on a warm day and after separating the lambs from the mothers was a trying time. The noise in the pens was deafening and continued all through the first night.

One spring in the early 1990s, Brian and I were working near the out-buildings cleaning potatoes. It was mid to late May, we had settled down in the potato pit after doing the morning chores and we were separating out bad ones to rescue the final crop that had been in storage over the winter under grass turfs. Between lambing duties, we had cleaned a lot of the stock. After some time, Frances came down with some drinks and food and noticed we were really burnt by the sun. A mixture of enclosed area and a cool breeze had led us into a false security over the sun's rays. But we coped with the tender skin the next day. I cannot remember another time so early in the season when sunburn was an issue!

One late morning we heard of a local disaster not far from us. A lorry going to the market in Lairg had come off the road. The crate on the back was not secured properly against the truck and when the truck went round the corner, near Rhaoine, west of Muie and Acheilidh, the crate flipped off and a lot of lambs died or were put down later by the vet. A lady was killed in the incident. It was a very sad day for us.

Another early start was the day of the lamb sales. I used Lairg Mart for many years. Rogart had closed some time back in company reshuffles. Two sales early and late were the opportunities to show off the lambs and hopefully get good prices. The later sales historically seemed to give better prices and more stable bidding. But the market forces and even the number of people wanting to buy had an impact on the prices. With the years rolling by, it was reassuring that one person was always at the sales carrying out guard duty at the pens leading to the ring. Davy Snody was a well-known face by all and a man with a mission. Sadly, he died many years ago.

Evidently the good shepherds and farmers or crofters fared well most years. Certain buyers looking out for their favourite sellers would have travelled across the country, even over the English border, to buy hardy hill sheep that could strengthen the park lambs of the south in the breeding from as far north as where we were.

My preference was to be in the early batches and separate the selling lambs into small groups whereby the buyers could test the prices and I might get a better average price. I tried in the earlier years to put Frances round with the lambs in the ring hoping that might help the price! I had done reasonably well most years and considering the general prices I was thankful for the prices I obtained. The last thing I wanted to do was to bring back lambs because the price was too low.

If it was a good day, anyway, the livestock driver would pick up the sheep, head off to Lairg to the sales pens on the south side of the village and I would follow on after. Once there, I would check things were all right and would check a few prices of sheep going through. Seeing the same faces yearly was somehow comforting, the buyers and sellers making their trips to the mart to carry out the business. The turnover was nothing like the numbers going back to the 1970s but the sale in Lairg was still one of, if not, the largest one-day sales in the country.

As the day went on, the regular occurrence of tea and pies for lunch went down well, especially when most years at this time the wind would have a chill to it. Willan Mackenzie from along our road past the Sutherlands was a definite pie and tea man. He was a real all-encompassing shepherd who looked after his flock almost like children. He would go through bags of feed over the winter. But when it came to the sales, buyers would pay a premium for his lambs. He repeatedly got prices over the average for 'tops' for his fine sheep.

Willan died some thirty years ago and we lost the best shepherd of the area. Ian Mackenzie (his nephew) took over croft after Willan. It was good also to meet up with locals and chat about the topics of the day leaning on fences and kicking the dust with our boots.

Once all done it was a short drive back to Acheilidh for dinner and a quick check around the croft before listening to some country dance music on the radio and another day done.

Jimmy Mackay of Acheilidh

When I consider who is left in Rogart, near Acheilidh, there are only Kathleen and Raymond Ross, (Geordie's wife and son) who live in Muie. Geordie would help me over the years, especially with providing his bull and I would walk the cow along the road to Muie for the bull to do his business. The MacLeods are gone (Alix was later in a care home in Dornoch) and the Sutherlands have moved twice since being in Rogart. The newcomers of Acheilidh croft, Donald and June, are now the longest serving people in the area.

The years have been kind to me. I am in a lovely place where the staff look after me by going the extra mile. I cannot believe it is over ten years since we left Acheilidh for Perth.

Like all the Mackays of Acheilidh, I am proud of my roots and heritage. It is encouraging to hear of many people with these same roots in Acheilidh making progress in all parts of the world.

I appreciate, as you do, all the work that Anne Beer has carried out to bring all these stories together in one place.

Mackays, Clan from the North of Scotland with Roots in the Moray Coast. Supporters of Robert the Bruce and Anti-Jacobite!

Let me finish with the Mackay motto: *Manu forti* (With a strong hand).

5. THE TORROBLE SIBLINGS

The stories here follow twelve siblings, all born in Torroble croft between 1875 and 1899. Half of them lived out the end of their lives abroad, in most cases doing well in various enterprises. Most were to find partners who were themselves not from Sutherland as they scattered to live in many different places across the world.

Elsie was the daughter of Christina Mackay (1853-1920) and Donald Mackay (1849-1932) who were, themselves, born locally: Christina in Balone and Donald in Torroble. I was told Christina lost two children soon after birth[8] – she bore

---

[8] There is some dispute over whether she lost one or two children. One of these children, at least, was named and is listed below.

fourteen children in all. She was often catering for fourteen people, including herself and her children. Once the family's carting business was flourishing, she had local girls come in to help with the immense daily task of keeping everything in order for such a large family and when the children started to leave home, she sometimes had live-in domestic servants to help keep the house. Imagine what that was like in the days before washing machines, vacuum cleaners, clothes dryers, refrigerators, piped water supply, and hot and drinking water on tap, with nothing other than coal-fired stoves for cooking and small fireplaces in the main rooms to keep the croft warm in winter.

Like many born in the Victorian period, Donald was apparently not an easy man to please and often expected too much of his children, particularly those who remained behind to assist on the croft. Perhaps understandably as so many of the boys had left to work abroad and the girls to work elsewhere in Britain, leaving insufficient labour to run the croft efficiently.

Christina died in 1920 at the age of sixty-six, well before her husband. It is hardly surprising, given that she gave birth to fourteen children and slaved all her adult life to feed, clothe, and train the twelve of them as they grew up on the croft, as well as herself and their father.

Elsie was one of the eldest and, like her siblings, was involved in the day-to-day running of the croft whilst completing her school education and taking on other local employment. The large size of the family meant they struggled financially as the children were growing up but, as Elsie's siblings finished school, many emigrated elsewhere to start new lives. After working in domestic service jobs at home and in the USA, Elsie returned to Sutherland. For five years, she worked helping her mother as many of her siblings had left home, as well as helping in other homes, including that of her cousin, Hector Mackay, who was later to inherit Sydney House from his father.

A new chapter of her life began when she married John Skinner of Wick and Lairg in 1910. My mother, Jean Macdonald Skinner, was her only daughter. Jean married Londoner Geoffrey Edward Beer during World War II and together they had three children: myself, Anne, Penelope Jane, and Ian.

The Torroble Siblings

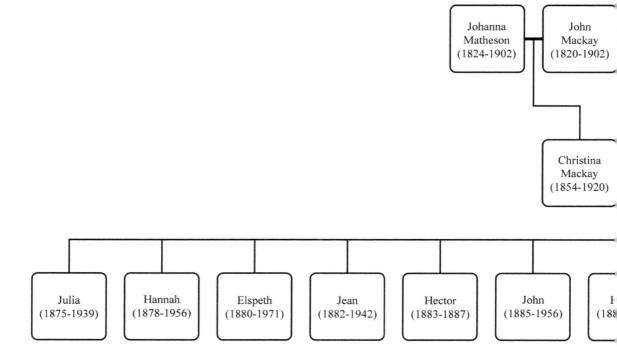

A section of the family tree of the Torroble Mackays.

The Torroble Siblings

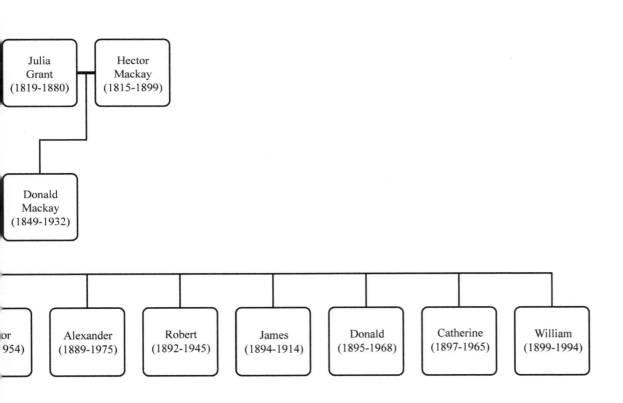

See Appendices B and E for more detail.

Julia

(1875 -1939)

Julia was the eldest child, born in 1875. She completed school in Lairg and, as with most of her siblings, did well. Gaelic was spoken at home but she was intent on leaving Lairg for a more interesting city life where good English would be essential. Through friends of the family, she found employment in an Edinburgh household as a domestic servant. Doing this as a first job was the norm for almost all girls from crofting families in those days – such work was seen as part of the education of girls so that they could learn more about how to run and manage a household, as well as the behaviours expected of young women in the Victorian era. She enjoyed her time in Edinburgh. In 1904, she married John Eric Campbell, who she first met in Lairg. John was from a local family and was the same age and similarly ambitious. They had two daughters and one son. Julia died in 1939 in Edinburgh.

Their first child was Margaret Ann Campbell – known to us as Meg. Meg married James (Jimmy) Campbell who earned his money as a senior banker at the Royal Bank of Scotland (RBS) but maintained a keen interest in Gaelic music all of his life. We have an old 1960s record of him singing but no device to play it on! We visited her and Jimmy in Northwood, north of London, fairly often.

Meg and James had three children – Fiona, Catherine, and Colin Campbell – but we have totally lost contact with them since their parents died.

Jimmy and Meg

Julia had two other children, Donald Mackay Campbell (1907-1948) and Hughina Mary Campbell (1913-1970). Donald married Ruby Morrison. Hughina married James Anderson Squair and they had two children, Bruce Donald (1948) and Ronald James (1950). Unfortunately, we have lost touch with these descendants.

Hannah

(1878-1956)

Having done well in her education at Lairg school, Hannah went on to train as a teacher in Edinburgh. This was at a time when the churches and the government were making efforts to increase the number of female teachers with special courses being set up to educate them. She taught in several schools, eventually moving to the mining village of Ashington in Northumberland.

Hannah married Ernest Bainbridge who was employed as an electrical engineer in the local coal mine. They had one son, Cyril, who was an exceptionally clever student and gained a place and scholarship at Glasgow University in the late 1930s to study medicine. He had started to practise as a doctor just as World War II was getting underway and inevitably was recruited into the army. However, he then

Hannah, attending one of the earliest teacher training
courses for women in Scotland

became the Medical Officer of Health for Glasgow, by which time he was living in Bearsden, north of Glasgow. He married Christine as the war was finishing but unfortunately she was not a well woman and for many years he dedicated his life to looking after her.

Elspeth (Elsie)

(1880-1971)

Elsie was the third child to Christina and Donald. Elsie left the family croft for a job in New York in 1897 and was fortunate to find herself working in a household of world renown. This was a rather extraordinary occurrence for a crofter's child, particularly in those times when the family was not well off, although they were by no means the poorest in their society, as they had the proceeds of their father's innovative carting business set up on their land when Lairg station was built next to their fields.

The change in fortunes for several of the Torroble children came when, one day, Elsie received an entirely unanticipated letter directly addressed to her from Andrew Carnegie – an American of Scottish descent and the wealthiest individual in the world at the time.

Andrew Carnegie's early work in founding businesses can be seen as the foundation for the technological emergence of the USA in the nineteenth century. He started from the bottom of society when he arrived in the USA as his parents, well-educated tradespeople producing handmade goods, had lost everything before deciding to leave the town of Dunfermline in central Scotland in 1835 to seek a new life. Andrew, working first in a textile firm as a bobbin boy, moved on to become a telegraph operator and then to work on some of the early train systems. It was there he became interested in iron and its production, using the Bessemer steel process first used in mass in Sheffield to produce cheap, high quality steel. This process revolutionised the building industry, as well as made the growth of railway systems possible. When he was almost forty years old, he founded Keystone Works which went on to become US Steel. For a time, he was the wealthiest person in the world but then he started giving much of his wealth away to good causes, as well as towards the education of the masses in the USA and Britain, and then elsewhere in the world.

The arrival of the letter was a seemingly unbelievable event but one she spoke of often. It seems most likely that she was recommended to Andrew Carnegie by one of the Highland hunting estate owners in the area of Lairg. Carnegie would have made the acquaintance of such estate owners as he rebuilt Skibo Castle near Dornoch on the east coast of Sutherland. He was intent on making this old Bishops's Palace into his own Highland home which, his letters show, he was doing to please his wife, Louise.

Once their only child, Margaret, was born in New York, the Carnegies appear to have decided they wanted a Highland lass to join their team of American nannies. Elsie, now seventeen years old, had helped her mother bring up at least nine babies by then. She was often on baby duty once she was of a certain age, looking after them, as well as helping other local families look after sick children or those that needed watching over. She probably knew more about babies than any American nanny just because of that! It was this experience with children which earned her her job with the Carnegies. Her skill with babies meant Elsie had frequent contact with both the Carnegies to discuss concerns about their daughter.

Following the letter's instructions, she took the train from the Lairg to Skibo. She was almost too young to be scared by the situation and said she had a really good chat with the Carnegie parents and was delighted to be taken on. One of her favourite memories in New York was taking Margaret to Coney Island in her pram with several members of staff to protect them.

She travelled back and forth to New York several times and survived well in her interesting job, spending almost four years with the child in both Skibo and in the Carnegie household in New York. She was there in New York when their new mansion was being built but she left when the baby reached the stage of needing a governess rather than any nanny. My sister and I were to benefit from Elsie's experience with babies when living with her in Lochinver.

During that time, she got to know many of the permanent household staff – and there were a *lot* of staff working in the Carnegie household. She made good lasting friendships with some. That said, she was always silent on the subject of friends she made in the USA. I suspect the 'proper' nannies, feeling usurped, made life difficult for her at first but Elsie was charming by nature and found ways around issues very easily. She never said she was anything other than well-treated there.

It was the friendships she made amongst the permanent staff which enabled her to ask if her old staff contacts knew of any vacancies that might suit two young and energetic Scotsmen when her younger brothers, Alexander and Hector, decided to emigrate to the USA around 1910.

Having never before had anything to do with upper-class families in Victorian society, an era when class was everything, Elsie learned a great deal about the behavioural patterns of the different strata in society from her time with the Carnegies. This was a particularly formal time at the end of the Victorian and beginning of the Edwardian period. The Carnegie's child, Margaret, had her own servants to look after her part of the house and, from them, Elsie learned much about the mores of the time.

Louise Carnegie, who Granny felt liked her, was particularly kind to her. Louise encouraged her to observe how things were to be done correctly in their home – from the wearing and preparing of clothes to the laying of tables for banquets. She learned from Louise and her servants how the rich women of that period changed their clothes for every meal of the day and how they would need their clothes properly looked after by being laundered and pressed (ironed) before being returned to their rooms. She learned what was appropriate for the guests, as well as the servants they would bring. These personal servants would be expected to stay in the servants' quarters. Clothes had to be ironed so that they hung properly and the servants were expected to help their masters and mistresses in and out of their clothes. To us now, it all seems an unbelievable palaver.

She was also encouraged by Louise to sit on the stairs above the dining rooms both in the Skibo and New York houses and watch how the service was carried out. Elsie was particularly interested in clothes and was fascinated by what they wore, as well as how individuals interacted with people from different levels in society. Watching all these magnificently dressed visitors sitting in candlelight, often eating with music in the background, must have been like going to the cinema was for my generation. For a country girl, it was a real spectacle and one she used to tell us about over fifty years later.

Elsie (1910)

For a crofter's daughter, the experience was the equivalent of a university course today! Louise took her role in training her staff seriously – something Granny was to benefit from when she had staff of her own while running the Culag Hotel later in life.

For a time, Elsie came to know, if fleetingly, certain sections of the richest society of the USA and the U.K. We remember Granny showing us the Tiffany brooch Louise Carnegie gave her when she finished working for them. It never went to her head as she always thought of herself as a servant of others. This was perhaps due to her Presbyterian training at school – all Scottish schools in her time had church ministers whom Elsie deeply disliked. However, she received a good education and, by the time she left for the USA, her English had improved and she knew how to speak with Andrew Carnegie. This also helped when she served affluent society while working for the Duke and Duchess of Sutherland.

What Elsie learned working for the Carnegies was something few others in the north of Scotland would have had much idea about. Elsie never explained how she felt about her meetings with world famous people, only that it changed her expectations and her life totally. She was only seventeen years old from a relatively poor community and suddenly being spoken to by the world's richest with whom she would otherwise never had had cause to converse.

In her twenties, after she returned from about four years in America, Elsie was back at the family croft again, tending the land, looking after her younger siblings, taking on other local work, and helping her father with the carting business. Work was often quite fluid for young women like Elsie who had stints in various roles until she settled down. It appears Elsie sometimes went to work in other households when not needed on the croft, as can be seen in the census data where she was noted as being in another croft, looking after someone who was sick. At the time, there was really no other legitimate way women could get paid work in a crofting community other than being occasional servants in the homes of those better off.

Elsie's life changed substantially at the point that she married and began to run a hotel with her husband, John Skinner, which she did for the next thirty-five years. The knowledge learned from her time working for the Carnegies made it possible for her, a crofter's daughter, to contemplate running this business which had been designed in 1909 to be the most exclusive hotel in the northern Highlands[9].

Elsie was also a suffragette and used to show my sister and me her member's ribbon of purple, white, and green. As a result, we were brought up as strong feminists!

---

[9] Elsie's life is continued in 7. The Culag Years (1910-1946) (p.169).

Elsie and John Skinner

Jean

(1882-1942)

Jean   Innaeas Mackay

Jean was born in 1882. After finishing school and helping her mother run the household, she also worked as a domestic. When WWI broke out, she worked to help neighbours with harvesting and looking after their houses – the shortage of manpower meant women had to work in the fields to compensate for the drop in available labour due to the recruitment and then high death rate of soldiers, particularly amongst Highland boys.

Jean met a New Zealander soldier, Innaeas Mackay (b.1888 in Longbush, Southland) whom she married in 1918, going with him to New Zealand where he held land. Innaeas was an Acheilidh Mackay. His father, James Mackay (1830-1904) was also Jean's great uncle. In 1856, James was one of the first settlers in Southland, New Zealand. After 1868, he was followed by his three nephews John, Alexander and William from Balone. They farmed in Otama and Riversdale, Southland. Further descendants followed from later generations of Acheilidh Mackays.

In the 1960s, Jean and Inneas were living in Dunedin, New Zealand. Their daughter, Chrissie Jean (1922-2008) married Frederic P.A.J. Ransom and together they had a son, Ross Anthony Ransom (1947-2009) and a daughter, Heather Lorraine Ransom. Chrissie died in Dunedin.

Hector

(1883-1887)

The first Hector died in early infancy in January 1887 as a result of enteric fever.

John

(1885-1956)

John, born in 1885, was regarded as the first son and, as such, the child who would inherit the right to be the leaseholder of the buildings and the associated land. John seems to have been more taciturn than the other brothers – perhaps conscious of his position in the family. However, he too decided to leave Scotland, not long after Elsie returned from working in New York. North America was generally seen as being the land of opportunity to crofters' children in northern Scotland at the time and John wanted to see if he could make a better life for himself there. Opportunity was something that many young men felt was missing for them at home, with the land they lived on still controlled by landowners and the ever-present memories of land reallocation measures imposed right up to 1850 that affected so many of their grandparents and great-grandparents.

John arrived in Canada in 1907, after a short stay in Buffalo in New York State. He was registered as a carpenter, claiming Vancouver as his destination. He may have found work on the west coast, either as a carpenter or in farming, making use of skills he acquired at the croft. Being exceptionally strong and a willing worker, he would have easily found work. It is not clear how long this first transatlantic stay lasted before he returned to Scotland again.

John must have decided there were still likely to be better opportunities in the USA than at home. Sailing on the *Caledonia* from Glasgow, he arrived in New York in April 1911 with a cousin, Alexander Murray from Rogart, and a friend, Alexander Sutherland from Lairg. This time, he was claiming farm labour as his calling.

He found employment on John Tobin's ranch in Birdseye in Lewis and Clark County, Montana. The Tobins were relatively recent immigrants from Ireland – a large family started by Richard and Mary Tobin who emigrated from County Cork in the 1860s.

It is unclear how the young men ended up in Lewis and Clark, only a week or so after arriving in New York. Perhaps John had already been there on his first trip in 1907 or perhaps they were inspired by Buffalo Bill, who did a grand tour of Scotland in 1904, as far north as Inverness[10]. Little Bighorn is not far from the Tobin ranches.

---

[10] Tom F. Cunningham's 2008 book, *Your Fathers the Ghosts: Buffalo Bill's Wild West in Scotland* details Buffalo Bill's travels around Scotland.

The Torroble Siblings

Ella Tobin, possibly with John (right)

The Tobin family

Ella Tobin (second from left) and Alexander Murray (fifth from left, barely visible)

Unfortunately, these low-quality images are the only photographs we have of John's life in Montana.

From John's naturalisation application and the US federal census in 1920 we know he was employed as a ranch hand and then a foreman on the Tobin ranch for at least ten years. As a US citizen, John was liable to be drafted when the country entered World War I in April 1917 but his US draft registration card in 1918 shows he was suffering from partial paralysis of his right side. He presumably got injured while working at the ranch, making him able to work as a foreman but not as a ranch hand.

John's cousin, Alexander Murray, married John Tobin's sister, Ella, in 1922 with John Mackay was his witness. Alexander settled in Montana until his death in 1964. John continued to work as a rancher and was still shown as such on the passenger list when he went back to Scotland in October 1925. He may have gone back to the USA after this and might well have acquired some land there, but John's widowed father was growing older and needed help in running the croft.

John's brother, Donald, and his wife, Elizabeth, had been his father's main support in this period, but we know John had returned to live at the Torroble croft and to help run the coal merchant business by the time of his wedding to his cousin, Annie Macdonald Murray, Alexander's sister, in August 1929.

John's wife, Annie, and father Donald

It wasn't possible for the two married brothers and their wives to share the croft. Donald and Elizabeth had had two children by 1928 and by the time of the birth of his third child, he had moved to a house in Lairg and later to Gordonbush near Brora.

As John grew older, with all the economic difficulties of the period around World War II, with improved roads and lorries becoming more common, the carting business had gradually become less financially viable. So, John decided to capitalise on the still profitable coal business and passed it on to his young cousin, Hugh Macdonald, who had been working with John since he left school. Elsie was upset and felt that this was a mistake as she realised what a difference the income had made to her family's life before they left home.

John used the gains to supplement what was left of the little he had managed to bring back from the US. His remaining funds went to pay for himself and Annie to live as comfortably as they could in the home by now rather rundown from my own memories of our last visit in 1954. This visit greatly distressed Elsie, although she was totally unwilling to talk to us children of her feelings about seeing her old home so rundown. Our mother was there too and I remember them being worried about John's health and how the family croft was not being well looked after.

John was no longer the fit man of his youth. Due in part to the injuries suffered at the ranch and to heart disease, he could no longer move the large loads he had handled with ease in his youth. Given also that Annie was a practising teacher, not a crofter, it is little wonder that the croft had been left to decay.

John died in 1956, aged 71, shortly after our last visit. Annie died in 1963. Based on a newspaper article about him and Annie, it seems John was well-liked. Unlike Elsie, John was a very strong attender of church and a member of the Free Church. He was also a keen Freemason, as were many crofters and businessmen in the Lairg area and elsewhere in Sutherland at that time. The Freemasons were very strong after the war in rural areas of Scotland. Elsie's husband was also a keen supporter in his later years.

Hector

(1887-1954)

Hector was born in 1887. In Torroble, he worked as a clerk at the local railway company in Lairg, running a line from Inverness to the towns in northeast Sutherland, whilst also helping his father on the croft. As a boy, he was known to be good with figures – a skill that became even more apparent when working with the railway company. However, he had come to the conclusion that there were better prospects in the USA.

He left Scotland in the early 1900s with his brother, Alec, bound for the USA. With the help of Elsie's friends in the employ of the Carnegie family, he found good employment. His first job in the USA was as a junior servant in the White House in the time of President Taft (1909-1913). It was a very unusual first job for any immigrant and really only makes sense as a result of an introduction from one of Elsie's New York friends to a senior member of the White House housekeeping staff. Being highly organised, he was very quickly able to rise to become the Butler for the State Banqueting Room. He served in the US Army in WWI and was deployed to France.

He was intent on doing better and, after the war, he found that he had enough money to take a course in Insurance and Accounting. His studies in accountancy enabled him to get work as a junior member of staff for the Metropolitan Insurance Company of New York. He eventually became the general manager for the Long Island branch and did very well. He also found a very supportive wife in Lavinia Cumming (1885-1960), born in Moffat.

Like Alec, he frequently visited his sisters in Scotland and England, at least until he moved to Edinburgh. As children, we remember waving our great-uncles off on transatlantic liners leaving from Liverpool in the 1950s and 1960s. Both Hector and Alec would also visit their cousin, Hector, at Sydney House – often when their sisters, Hannah, Kate, and Elsie, also came to Lairg for family get-togethers. He left many of us with presents of plates as a memento of the time he worked in the White House. He said these plates were from President Taft's time and had been found at auction.

Unfortunately, Hector became ill and retired in 1952 and he and Lavinia returned to Edinburgh. Hector died in 1954. After his death, Lavinia remained in Edinburgh. She died in 1960.

Alexander (Alec)

(1889-1975)

Alec was born in 1889. He was a naturally quick learner and, although a Gaelic speaker at home like all his siblings, he had a thorough, if fairly basic, education to the age of thirteen, including in the English language. Alongside his education at the local school in Lairg, Alec worked on their father's croft, looking after the animals – particularly the horses which were used in his father's carting business, as well as for ploughing.

Alec's first jobs after school were as a farmhand working locally in Lairg for other crofters as well as his father but, by the time he was about seventeen years old, he knew he needed to do more with his life.

Alec's first stint working away from home was as a seaman on the *S.S. Claymore*, a Scottish West Coast Steamer, providing a delivery service up and down the west coast of Scotland and its islands, calling at coastal towns and villages. It was an area that was barely serviced by cross country roads – rough tracks at best in the days before there were more vehicles on the road. He had learned on the farm about making tools and modifying them and those skills proved useful while working on the coastal boats as a seaman. In that period, he got to know the city of Glasgow well and enjoyed the busy life there far more than life at home in Lairg village. Free of family disapproval and control, Alec, like any young man, enjoyed city life.

His brother, Hector, decided to join him and, after a time in Glasgow, the two set out together for New York. All this emigration of crofting children led to a very real dearth of labour, magnified by the occurrence of World War I, when so many crofters' sons died.

With contacts there from their sister's time in the city, they soon found employment. These particular contacts in prestigious establishments gave Alec his way in, as the people he was to work for knew the Carnegie family.

Elsie's staff network, those serving the very rich of New York, found a vacancy for Alec in the Bostwick Family – yet another of the wealthiest in the world in that pre-WWI period. There was a household vacancy for a young valet and, with that, Alec had his foot in the door.

Over the decades, Alec rose to become the factor (estate manager) for the Bostwicks who lived in a mansion not far from the Carnegie's. Also nearby were close friends the Rockefellers whose mansion was at No. 4 West 54th Street. The Bostwicks also had a chateau in France; stables for polo ponies in the Butternut Valley in the small town of Gilbertsville, not far from the Rockefeller's upstate New York estate; and a house in Aitken, North Carolina for the winter months.

It was in Aitken that we believe he met his wife, Helen Daniels, an American citizen from that area. Alec and Helen had houses in both Aitken and Gilbertsville. Helen was a school teacher. Like many of our extended family, we visited them there in both homes in the 1970s and 1980s – they were very hospitable.

Alec interacted regularly with both the Rockefellers and the Bostwicks on a personal level at various horse events as both families were horse owners – the Rockefellers of racehorses and the Bostwicks of polo ponies, in particular, although they had other horses too. Alec was not an employee of the Rockefellers but did work with their horses through their shared interests and used to meet with them and their staff fairly regularly when young.

Both the Bostwicks and Rockefellers were involved in the Standard Oil Trust, a business which, in 1880, held ninety percent of American refining capacity and so made both families the wealthiest in the USA except for the Carnegies. The Bostwicks and Rockefellers knew Andrew Carnegie well and their townhouses were near his in New York City. All these families were to give away considerable proportions of their wealth to good causes and charitable projects to improve the life of the masses over many decades. They socialised together frequently.

Rockefeller and Carnegie were also friends with Henry Phipps. The Phipps family had dealt with Carnegie's massive purchases of various businesses, legitimately profiting themselves from the deals they organised. So much so that they themselves bought the rights to the Bessemer steel process from him – the process which revolutionised steel production by greatly speeding up manufacture and profitability. Alec was personally known to both Henry and Ogden Phipps. It was the latter who allowed Alec to use their New York apartment for our parents, Jean and Geoffrey Beer, when they visited New York as part of their family visit to Alec and Helen in New York and Aitken in the 1970s.

Alec with his favourite horse

Surprising perhaps that a self-effacing boy, brought up on a small croft in a remote village could so easily fit in to the job of managing the large acres of land accumulated by the richest in the USA in the early 1900s.

Alec was employed by the Bostwicks for most of his life and spent the rest of his life in the USA with the exception of military service in France and holidaying in Britain to visit relatives that remained there. He also made regular short trips to France post-WWI to work in the Bostwick's chateau, not far from Paris.

Helen and Alec

All his life, Alec loved antiques and whenever he visited our mother, he would bring something. I still have the incense burner he gave to her.

Alec was well regarded for his estate management skills. He died before Helen, in 1975. Helen eventually moved down south in the USA, mainly to avoid northern winters. She sold the Aitken house and had an apartment in Florida where she was well cared for by her own relatives, the Moores, whom we never met, unfortunately. She died in 2002.

Robert

(1892-1945)

Prior to emigrating to the USA, Robert helped out on the croft. In the early 1900s, he was sent by his father to work in the first garage in Lairg. There he learned all about looking after and driving motorised vehicles, including how to service the new fangled motor cars.

Upon moving to New York these skills helped Robert find employment with the telephone company and he soon proved himself to be a well-organised young man. He married Katherine Grieve and they moved to the Bronx. He soon advanced to become the supervisor of lines in the Bronx area. Robert died in 1945, from heart disease and failure. Katherine apparently lived until 1987.

James

(1894-1914)

Following his education at Lairg school, James was sent to Golspie High School. He did very well at school, finding work afterwards in a solicitor's office in Golspie until he contracted typhoid fever from which he died in February 1914 in Cambusavie Hospital, Golspie.

Donald

(1895-1968)

Donald was born on 31 December 1895 and, like the other children, grew up first playing on the croft and was later well-educated at Lairg School. On finishing school at the age of thirteen, he started to work full-time with his father. In effect, learning the skills necessary to be a crofter served as an apprenticeship in land and animal management. His father increasingly needed help, as the older boys in the family left home from 1907 onwards – there was simply not enough labour for all the farm work that needed doing, from looking after crops to handling the general maintenance around the house. Additional labour must have been brought in to help with outside work, as well as the family carting business which was their main source of income. Extra labour was needed for outdoor work, in particular, to help Christina in the house – one census shows two domestic servants working on Torroble croft around the time Christina started to become ill.

At the beginning of WWI in 1914, before the age of twenty, Donald was recruited into the army. He began training with his regiment, the Seaforth Highlanders, in Perthshire. This again exacerbated the lack of labour available on the croft and inevitably meant the girls were expected to do more – but, by then, only the youngest sister, Kate, was still at home.

Following his training, Donald was serving overseas in France when he was gassed. Following this incident, he spent some time in hospital in Scotland before being discharged to civilian life. When he was allowed to return home, he was not fully recovered. That young Donald was gassed during WWI was something that affected him for the rest of his life although he continued to work in spite of it.

While recuperating from his injuries, Donald met and married his wife, Elizabeth Hepburn Dunn (1898-1972). They had three daughters and two sons. His eldest two daughters, Chris and Jenny, were the last Mackays to be born at Torroble croft in 1922 and 1925 respectively.

By the time Donald returned to Torroble croft, his mother was unwell and also required help. Following her death in 1921, father Donald required his help with both the croft and the carting business. Working with his father to keep the croft going, Donald looked after the animals and the crops and brought the oats and barley to the Lairg millers after organising, cutting, and gathering it into stooks. Donald also managed the running of the family's delivery and, later, coal merchant's business, taking goods delivered to and from Lairg Station across to the west coast villages and to areas north of Lairg.

As his father became less capable of the hard physical work, Donald only had his wife and very young children to help him. Without his hard work, the croft would not have even been able to support the remaining family. As Donald's father continued to age, young Donald had, in reality, done all the work to run the croft for a decade or more. The major change he made while doing this was to build up the coal merchant's side of the carting business which gradually became the main source of income.

On his elder brother, John's return to Torroble, Donald continued to help around the croft for several years but they had very different ideas about how things should be run. Gradually – almost inevitably – it became too difficult in the croft with Donald's family. Eventually, Donald decided he and his wife and two children would move to live in Lairg. To be able to support his own family, Donald had to find other work.

Donald   Elizabeth Hepburn Dunn

He was fortunate to find work on an estate near Brora on the east coast, just over twenty miles away. It was a land management job with a house that went with it. There, he was part of a small team looking after a gentleman's deer stalking and fishing estate owned by the Tyser family. The estate specialised in providing salmon fishing, grouse shooting, and deer hunting for the very well-off visitors from the south. The

Tyser family was one of Scotland's richest families at the time. The Tysers purchased the Brora estate in 1921 from the Sutherlands when they were beginning to run into financial problems.

Donald and Elizabeth's sons, Hamish and Alistair, were born in Brora. The house on the Brora estate was an ideal family home. His wife and young family thrived there while he enjoyed looking after the land and wildlife, in particular the horses.

When WWII began in 1939 Donald was given notice to leave his job as the Tyser estate was closed down for visitors and the owners had other priorities to survive the wartime period. For Donald this presented a problem of where to live. The seemingly logical choice to return to Torroble was not possible as his relationship with John remained difficult. Elsie was always angry about what happened between the two brothers but never explained the details to us children – only talking to us in her nineties about how unfair the situation was for Donald and his family.

With another child on the way, they had to hurry to find somewhere to live. The only place they could find was in Gruids, a relatively remote hamlet near Lairg where they were able to rent an old cottage. It was not much more than a bothy, with no modern amenities, including no running water. Their youngest daughter, Elizabeth, was born into this rundown cottage. It appears John and his wife provided no assistance in making the cottage more liveable.

Donald was virtually unemployed for a time, doing odd jobs to keep the family fed. He also had some longer-term jobs on other crofts and estates around the area, including Sallachy Lodge. Donald joined the local home guard, manning a telephone box in the evenings for several hours at a time.

In December 1939, the family moved to a council house overlooking the shores of Loch Shin and Donald took up work as caretaker of the local school in Lairg. This was to be the family home for the rest of his life. He became very involved in the local community and was well-liked. He was instrumental in setting up the collection of old newspapers during the war years and for some time after. They were sold on for cash to help the youngsters of the village in the difficult wartime and post-war years. Donald was a founding member of the local football club, creating a full-sized pitch with the help of local contractors. His love of fishing (free on Loch Shin at that time) led to a little side business of letting out boats to locals and tourists alike and would eventually lead to the formation of the angling club.

All his married life Donald never strayed very far from home but it was his ambition upon retirement to visit his younger brother, Bill, in New Zealand. He set sail on his own in 1961 and was warmly welcomed on arrival by his numerous relatives there, many of whom he had never met before. It was on his return that he became involved in tracing some of the Acheilidh Mackay history for Bill.

The remainder of his retirement years were spent quietly in Lairg: fishing, bowling, and gardening. A stroke in the early 1960s curtailed those activities to a some extent.

Donald and Elizabeth's children went on to have families of their own. Their youngest daughter, Elizabeth, has been in touch as part of this project[11]. She is still fit and healthy and lives with her husband, Colin, in the southwest of England.

Catherine (Kate)

(1897-1965)

Kate was born in 1897. After school, Kate attended The School of Domestic Science in Atholl Crescent in Edinburgh to train as a domestic science teacher. However, while there, she became more interested in hotel management. She worked in several establishments in Edinburgh before taking a job as a housekeeper of a large estate specialising in hunting and breeding horses. The wife of the estate owner, Tommy

---

[11] Elizabeth's contributions are continued in 8. Later Generations: The Enduring Mackay Line, p.217.

Tommy and Kate's wedding (1931)

Robson, became very ill and died while Kate was running the domestic side of things. Sometime later, she married Tommy and took over the running of the Dunstanburgh Castle Hotel. The hotel continued to be popular with people visiting the spectacular coast of the Dunstanburgh area of Northumberland, as well as with golfers.

Kate with her son, Alistair   Alistair Robson

They handed the hotel over to their son, Alistair Robson, when they became ill. Alistair then ran it with his wife, Judy, a woman from Jesmond, Newcastle with a similar interest in horses, for some years after Kate and Tommy died. Eventually, Alistair sold it, mainly because he much preferred dealing with horses to hotel staff and guests. His now ex-wife, Judy, still lives adjacent to the hotel and is in contact with the family.

William (Bill)

(1899-1994)

After leaving school, William joined the army in 1916 and trained with the Argyll and Sutherland Highlanders at Dunfermline and Redford barracks in Edinburgh. Once drafted to France in 1917, he was transferred to the Black Watch and the 51st division on the Somme. It was one of the worst battles of the First World War and an event which can only have been totally traumatic for such a young man. After the Somme, he spent a further year in France before being demobilised.

He then took a course at Skerry's College in Edinburgh, before finding a job in the post office for a short time. In 1921, he wisely decided to leave for New Zealand where he married Isabella. They had two daughters: Mildred and Dorothy.

Dorothy lives in Christchurch, New Zealand with her husband. She ran a very successful clothes business there for many years. Their daughter, Nicky, now in her sixties, lives with them. Mildred had two sons and six daughters, including

Donna, whom we knew well from her visits to Britain which continued into the 1980s. I visited her twice in Melbourne, Australia. The last of these visits was sadly just before she died. Donna had two children who were still young when I met them– now adults themselves but we have unfortunately lost contact over the years. Bill's other grandchild, Cheryl, lived in Auckland and has often visited relatives in Britain.

Bill, Isabella, Mildred, and Dorothy

The Torroble family

L-R: Julia, Hector, Jean, Donald, James, John, Donald, Christina, Robert, Hannah, Alec, and Elspeth.

Lochinver in winter

Lochinver in winter

Lochinver in winter

6. LOCHINVER

An essay written in 1965 by Jean Skinner, our mother, on the Lochinver of her childhood. It describes the village and the surrounding area as it was from when she was born in 1917 up to 1947.

Lochinver is a small village situated on the west coast of the county of Sutherland, not far south of Cape Wrath. It is built around the margin of a sea-loch which is almost completely enclosed by two headlands. To the landward is an irregular horseshoe of hills of grey gneiss rock and heather; these rise almost immediately from the bay and stretch back into the gradually rising hinterland, out of which emerges a panorama of six mountain peaks of striking shape: Quinag, Canisp, Suilven, Cul Mor, Cul Beag, and Stac Pollaidh. It is a configuration only fully visible from the sea. The climate is wet but mild under the influence of the Gulf Stream.

Lochinver

This land formation has left only a narrow coastal shelf where, following the line of the shore and very close to the sea, the village has been built with a line of houses as far as the northern headland. The main street stretches for a mile between two bridges, one at each end of the base of the horseshoe. The bridges cross the River Inver, a salmon river, at the north end and the Culag Burn at the south. At the Culag Bridge, the road forks left for the school and the coast road to

Ullapool, and right to the pier and the hotel, which are situated a little way along the southern headland.

Almost all the houses and shops face the bay. From those in the middle of the winding street, the Isle of Lewis can be seen between the headlands when the weather is clear.

In the village, there are two general stores selling almost everything from food to salmon and trout flies as well as a post office and the bank. In the 1930s, there was also a painter and decorator, a plumber, a mason, and a joiner – in short, everything required to make the place self-sufficient. No doubt some of these remain but several shops have long since disappeared.

The main occupation of the village, even in the 1950s, was still fishing. This grew into a major industry in that period, centred on the pier with its modern freezing plant. The tourist industry, too, remained important and visitors continued to come to the hotel every summer for trout and salmon fishing.

By the 1960s, many more motorists were finding their way north and private houses began to cater for bed and breakfast. There were still some crofts in the outlying areas but the land had always been poor and infertile and most crofters had to go fishing or lobster fishing to supplement the income from their sheep. They used also to go gillying: the practice of local expert fishermen taking visitors out to the local rivers to catch salmon and trout. This occupation gradually died down as the older generation of visitors ceased to come, resulting in there no longer being enough work for the local gillies.

Lochinver Bay

Up to the 1950s, many yachts used the bay as anchorage in summer. Trawlers from Grimsby and Fleetwood, as well as drifters from Banff and Buckie, came to the pier for shelter in stormy weather. There used to be a regular cargo boat from Glasgow but this stopped long ago.

I got to know the village from the backdrop of the hotel which my parents kept for thirty years, originally a shooting lodge belonging to the Duke of Sutherland. That first building was destroyed by fire in 1929 and was substantially bigger than the present building.

The Culag Hotel today

I can still see it clearly: a building with large public rooms with panels in Pitchpine; a Pipers gallery; long corridors. It was heaven for a child to play in the public area of the hotel on winter nights when the wind howled, the shutters rattled, and the candle in my bedroom threw grotesque and frightening shadows.

The sea seemed almost part of the house. During a storm, when the bay was lashed to a grey and white fury and the gulls wheeled and balanced on the wind, the spindrift used to lash at our windows, leaving a trail of seaweed on the terrace.

Thinking about it, the past comes back to me in random flashes – it is summer now and the hotel is full of guests. Evenings in the front hall, there are trays of trout and one or two of salmon which the gillies have arranged so that the catches can be commented upon and admired. The smell is distinctive: fish, rubber boots, and wet waterproofs.

Black Niall and Big Roddy are talking in Gaelic and packing salmon in green rushes. When they have finished, it will look like a miniature green zeppelin and go off on the morning mail car to the south. Both Niall and Roddy work small crofts and live in Inverkirkaig. A winding, three mile walk from the village which will take them past the village school.

It is a picturesque and unusual school that stands on a little peninsula in the middle of the Culag Loch, with no other house in sight. Near it is an island which the children can reach by stepping stones when the loch is not too high and a sloping rock, polished smooth by countless sliding bottoms – a permanent invitation to successive generations of children to come and wear out their trousers, too. There is a playground but it is used more by sheep than by children – after all, what need is there of any playground when burns, hills, and woods are all around?

The road home from the school follows the burn past the old mill and down to the sea again. In the autumn, when the heather is out on the hills and the rowan berries red, we pick and eat the milky white hazelnuts on our way. At that time of year, the burn is often in spate and makes huge yellow foam pancakes which lie in the eddies.

Rowans, hazels, and birches are the indigenous trees but a kind of a forest has been grown on the heath land behind the hotel. A carved stone inscription on a rock bears witness: "these woods were planted and these piles made by George Granville, second Duke and twentieth Earl of Sutherland". Here, the trees grow thick and the air is hushed and mysterious as we follow the winding route, a gnarled path. The sound of our footsteps deadened by the pine needles. In the shade grow tall red and white foxgloves and all sorts of fairy toadstools. In the spring, violets and wood-sorrel, a band in the soft green moss, and primroses by the trickling water runnels. The path leads to the sea again to a shingly beach known locally as White Shore Mor[12]. It was a place where hotel guests and villagers bathed in the summer.

Another memory from my life at the Culag: the Claymore is tied up at the pier, unloading its cargo from Glasgow. Steamer day is always an event in the village, bringing cars, vans, and lorries from the outlying districts to collect the goods. All is bustle and noise and I can still hear the unmistakable rattle of the ship's derrick and the shouts

---

[12] The place Jean's ashes were scattered in April 1982.

of "lower away!" as the goods are lifted out of the hold and onto the pier

How can any but a poet conjure up the whole atmosphere of the place? The heather honey of the hills, the soul and grandeur of the mountains, and the peaceful lap of the water against the boat side when fishing on a lonely loch. The melancholy crying of the seagulls, sad and haunting as the air of a Gaelic song, the smell of the peat smoke from the houses, and the kindly hospitable folk.

Lochinver

Culag Loch School

7. THE CULAG YEARS (1910-1946)

The Culag is a building in the village of Lochinver, part of the Assynt district in the far northwest of Scotland, with spectacular landscapes that still grow wild. The Isle of Lewis can be seen clearly when looking west over Lochinver Bay.

Our grandfather always drew attention to it as that was where he said his mother had come from, having been born in Stornaway and then travelled to find work in Wick where she met John's father, who had a stonemason business there. For centuries, the Lochinver Bay had been used by passing boats as a safe haven in times of storm.

The Culag site was over the base of a much older building, one which had been constructed by The Macdonald (the Lord of the Isles) in the late eighteenth century. Centuries earlier a pier was built there, at the point where the sweet water from Loch Culag went into the sea, providing a useful supply of clean water for those preparing the fish for sale.

The Culag (c.1910)

The Culag was designed to function as a fish processing unit as it was near where herring, then in very plentiful supply, could be landed at a small pier on the edge of Lochinver Bay. The preserved herring would then be sent for sale in the burgeoning markets elsewhere in Britain and abroad. This was an increasingly profitable business at the time in northern Scotland, as evidenced by the growth of the town of Wick on the far northeast coast. The fish trade in Lochinver, while on a much smaller scale than Wick, was still profitable.

The fish that landed in Lochinver had to be gutted and then kippered (by drying over fires) or, alternatively, cured using salt and then sold on in jars. Both of these products were sent to the fish markets of the south and of northern Europe by sea, mainly going to Wick for export. The herring fishing industry was subject to great and uncontrollable fluctuations as the shoals of fish did not always appear in the same places ever year. Processing the herring when the fishing season was good benefited the crofters of the Assynt district and, at its heart, the village of Lochinver, by providing the possibility of extra income for local families.

The cleaning and preserving of the fish was mainly seen as a woman's job. At the height of the trade, many additional hands came to work in the village, particularly from the Western Isles. Women in general had increasingly begun to do some work in factories after WWI but always on much lower pay. It was really only from the 1950s that it became common in peacetime. There were no factories in the Highlands in the first half of the twentieth century – the nearest thing for women needing to work to survive was working as a fish-gutter on the herring catch, somewhere like Helmsdale or Wick. To us today, it would appear a fate worse than death – it really was an incredibly hard slog.

At the end of the nineteenth century, the Dukes decided to convert their fish processing building on the Culag site in Lochinver into a family hunting lodge, where they intended to invite their many affluent and influential friends from all over Britain and Europe to join them as guests to fish and hunt in the most beautiful scenery. The Sutherlands were among the richest in Britain and held a seat in the House of Lords. In late Victorian times, they would have known those who were generally thought to matter in British society. To us now, this seems ridiculously elitist but it was how society ran in a time of very cheap labour.

By the start of the twentieth century, the Sutherlands needed to raise income and one way to do that was to identify which areas of the land they owned might produce a higher level of income. Their idea to maximise profits was to convert the family hunting lodge, used to entertain friends as well as people they wanted to impress, into a hotel people paid to visit.

Finally, in 1929, the building suffered a major fire. When rebuilt, it was merely a shadow of its former self. Now very much smaller, the Culag Hotel no longer dominates the landscape but does still function as a hotel, catering for the many passersby following the North Scotland Cycle route which passes near Lochinver, as well as by walkers and other holiday-makers.

Redesigning the Culag

The hotel premises were adjacent to Lochinver Pier which, at the time, was on the coastal steamer weekly service from Glasgow to the Western Isles and northwest coast of Sutherland.

Setting up and investing in a hotel in such a remote location can only be seen, in retrospect, as a potentially reckless decision – even if one was, at the time, recognised as having been the richest family in Britain since the 1850s. Setting up hunting lodges and then hotels in the early 1900s, particularly in the days before motorised transport became common, now seems rather extraordinary – even if located in what was one of the most beautiful unspoilt landscapes in Britain. It is still exceptionally beautiful, if now in part spoiled by the village pier having been turned into a modern fish processing unit.

The Culag was in a very remote location, forty-five miles from the nearest station. The fourth Duke of Sutherland and his much younger wife, Duchess Millicent, decided to invest in making the structural changes to this building owned by the Sutherland estate. Some years earlier, the Sutherlands converted the building from an old smokehouse used to kipper herrings for export to the south of Scotland and England. Now, the fourth Duke had the idea that, once rebuilt, it could be used by their family as a hunting lodge, in the German hunting lodge style that was fashionable at the time, making it into a special place where they could entertain their friends from the south of England and abroad.

The original Culag buildings, which was used for the fish processing trade, were totally remodelled at the turn of the nineteenth century and designed in the classic Germanic hunting lodge style of the period. The dining room was kept from the hunting lodge days in the conversion to the Culag Hotel and stayed in use until the hotel burned down on Christmas Day 1929.

Their guests were to be well looked after and could enjoy various types of hunting with local men – gillies – all expert hunters and fishermen themselves. The gillies were there to locate the prey the guests were after.

It was a social success as far as the family was concerned but because of the changing economic circumstances of the early 1900s, the fourth Duke decided they should attempt to make some money out of the project. The family, which had not long before been the richest in Britain, had been heavily

CULAG HOTEL

Set in the sheltered shores of lovely Lochinver Bay amidst magnificent West Highland scenery, Culag Hotel (Culag means cosy corner) is an ideal fishing and residential hotel for those seeking a quiet and restful holiday.

Modern comforts, H. & C. in all bedrooms. Salmon and sea trout fishing on River Kirkaig, brown trout fishing on Loch Assynt, Loch Fionn and numerous other lochs. Sea fishing. Sporting rights reserved for hotel guests.

Bathing. Hill climbing.

Rail stations—Invershin 45 miles, Lairg 46 miles, Inverness 100 miles. Daily bus service from Lairg. Tariff—1st June-30th September, 10 to 14 gns. per week; remainder of year, 9 to 12 gns. per week. Brochure on request.

LOCHINVER

Phone: Lochinver 9   Grams: "Culag, Lochinver"

Advertisement for the Culag Hotel (1930s)

hit by taxes each time one of the Dukes died and they were in need of other sources of income.

The Dining Room at the Culag

Therefore, they decided to use their lodge as a hotel: one aimed at the well-off of the Edwardian era. A hotel for those wanting to hunt and fish; enjoy new landscapes; and be with people like themselves. These were particularly snobbish times in Britain, as a whole, as the new rich (the industrialist) and the old rich battled it out to be top dog. The old rich, of course, lost out, as they largely have done throughout history.

This meant the building had to be further modified so that it could better function as a hotel for paying guests.

The Culag

Having opened as a hotel in the early 1900s, the Duke's team then seem to have decided to look for someone from the region who knew about more than just running hotels and found that in our grandfather, John Ronaldson Skinner. John was a little different and also well-educated, someone used to dealing with the well-off and so having some real understanding of their requirements. He was, at least, someone with catering experience in the trade of keeping people happy.

The village football team, John Skinner seated front left

Having left school as Dux of the Academy (the brightest boy in the school) John started out in Wick as an articled clerk in a solicitor's office but quickly, and to his father's disappointment, found that boring. He left Wick for the Glasgow area and began, at about eighteen years old, training in the brewing industry. He ran public houses as part of his initial apprenticeship in the brewery trade. He was the chief brewer at a large Edinburgh Brewery just before he was offered the Culag job at the age of thirty. All went well after he completed his initial apprenticeship in Galashiels. We think he then moved from job to job, eventually working in small hotels where he began to be involved in catering, too. In that period of his life, he developed an easy way of talking with customers and guests, something which was useful to him when running a large hotel. He worked in Edinburgh and also Glasgow – in reality, always preferring city life.

Once initial discussions with the Duke's advisors started in 1909 in relation to the Culag job, it was quickly made clear he needed a wife. The type of hotel they envisaged needed someone to deal with the domestic part of running the hotel and someone aware enough of details to keep the ladies who were expected to visit happy, as well as someone who could run quite a large staff of men and women. There has always been a great deal of work behind-the-scenes in running any hotel, probably here made worse as the hotel, on the Duke's instruction, aimed to attract the highest in Edwardian Society. The Duke insisted everything be of the highest quality.

The job needed a woman with some understanding of the complex social etiquette of the period. John was lucky in that some of his family had left Wick not long after he did and moved to settle in Lairg to start a business. By then Lairg was a growing village connected to the south by the railway.

There, his brothers had got to know a local young woman, Elsie Mackay, whom they introduced to John. Elsie had been in the USA for several years working in a prominent and wealthy household.

By 1909 Elsie had been back in Lairg for several years after working for the Carnegie family for four years in the USA. Now in her late twenties she was helping her mother look after the land and the younger children who were still at home, as well as assisting her father with the carting business. John had already tried to persuade her to marry him in the early 1900s after she had returned from New York but she was ambitious and kept saying no to the idea.

She was the most sophisticated local woman he knew except for the big landowners as, having been part of the household of Louise and Andrew Carnegie, she had experienced a totally different world and developed an understanding of the very rich. John realised she would know how to please wealthy ladies and he understood what this might mean for running a successful hotel for the most well-off, as envisaged by the Duke and Duchess.

By the time the final offer was made to John to manage the Culag as its tenant, he seems to have got Elsie to agree to marry him. She was, at this stage, interviewed by Millicent, Duchess of Sutherland, who was well-known in the area where Elsie lived. She was always intent on 'doing good' by her husband's tenants – not something that went down well with Highland crofters! Elsie got on very well with her and was handed one of the signed photographs of Millicent which scattered the Highlands – Granny loved having it. It hung in her room for the rest of her life.

Elsie herself was very bright, too, and throughout her time in New York had watched and learned from what she observed. She understood just how the very affluent wanted to be treated; how they dealt with friends as well as servants like herself. How tables should be laid and food served. How to make a grand occasion for the ladies and gentlemen by the way rooms were prepared and the staff trained to behave. This etiquette, which might seem artificial to most of us ordinary individuals, was only to last until 1914 and the beginning of WWI. But for the first four years, the Culag did thrive as the Duchess had envisaged and she came fairly often to stay when her particular friends were visiting.

John and Elsie were both thirty years old when they married in Lairg on 14th December 1910. After the wedding, John had arranged a coach and horses to take them the forty-five miles over the hills to Lochinver. As dusk fell, they arrived to the point on the road to Lochinver where one got the first view of Lochinver Bay and the Culag building. Granny saw the whole building glow for he had arranged for every room in the hotel to have a candle in the window. Elsie was stunned. She never forgot this amazing sight of the hotel glowing in the dark. He was obviously a romantic!

Elsie and John on holiday in Monte Carlo (1925)

The Culag Hotel

John had signed the tenancy agreement with the Duke in August 1909. We still hold John's copy of the agreement to run the Culag. It sets out clearly what the owner was responsible for and what the proprietor, who used the building, had to look after at his own expense. It also laid out the hunting and shooting agreements for visitors using the land owned by the Duke, and how and by whom the land was to be cared for. The tenant was to pay an annual rent to use the building for guests but he was responsible for furnishing the building and all internal maintenance as well as its associated land. The early 1900s were, in economic terms, a time of great optimism in the U.K. and one can understand the Duke's line of reasoning. It was a time of great wealth among the landed gentry and business owners.

According to census data, there were thirty-seven rooms with a window in the building when it began operating as a hotel which seems optimistic in a remote hotel at that time. However, given that in Victorian and Edwardian times the well-off frequently took several of their own personal servants with them on such holiday jaunts, as opposed to housekeeping servants, this must have meant that, at any one time, more bedrooms were needed than just those for the actual guests. It also had a separate dining room for the visiting servants.

Initially there was little else in the village to interest the upper-class visitors of the time other than the enjoyment of sporting opportunities. So, the challenge for Elsie was to run the hotel in a manner in which the visiting women, in particular, would find there was something for them to do while their husbands were out hunting. A good number of the women made the effort to learn to fish; others went on walks accompanied by local guides; while others set off by pony and trap with local drivers to see the coastal scenery and picnic if the weather was kind. Beautiful, if rugged, scenery stretches both north and south from the hotel which, at the time, had its foundations in the sea. There was a constant lapping of water and, in wild weather, the noise of the waves hitting the rocks.

There was also a network of rough tracks and narrower paths to follow that led out from the hotel. Local guides could be arranged to take visitors to different viewpoints. Some went for long walks with guides carrying refreshments and showing guests the easiest routes around bogs and rocks – making it a different sort of holiday for the visitors from the south. Many little bays, like that at Inverkirkaig about four miles away, were easily accessible. Another sandy beach at Achmelvich, along the coast just north of Lochinver, was a favourite picnic place for guests and could be easily reached by pony and trap. Of course, the weather was an issue but the hotel had good drying rooms off of the warm kitchens for guests' use.

Within the grounds of the Culag Hotel, a short walk away, were woodlands and places where guests could picnic and swim in the sea. White Shore was a favourite location of our family. Our mother took us there frequently as young children to walk through the woods past a cliff face and to a place from which one could generate an echo if one shouted loud enough. After our mother's death in 1981, her ashes were scattered there in 1982 by her family, together with her very best friend from her Lochinver days, Helena Sutherland, MBE.

In retrospect, the Duke and Duchess's ideas were never going to be easy to implement, although, for a time, the hotel was a financial success and did attract the sort of clientele they had envisaged. The Duke's solution to run the building as a hotel in 1900 also still allowed for the fourth Duke and his wife on occasion to invite their own friends as guests to join them there for sporting activities on the surrounding hunting land.

For the hotel management and the staff, there was an enormous amount of work every day to keep to the agreed standards. In that time, before electric-run machinery, everything was down to manpower and all the staff had to understand what they were supposed to do at each part of the day to keep the customers happy. Water was probably piped into the house through clay pipes but it needed distributing by hand until the early 1920s when John Skinner invested in a system of lead piping and taps to provide water to all rooms. The source of this water is no longer known but it could well have been from Culag loch which lies several metres above the Culag building. Initially, however, moving water around could only be done by hard and frequent labour.

The bedrooms had to be set up and cleaned daily. The chamber pots, used in the days before flushing toilets were common, had to be emptied and kept clean. Drinking and warm water for washing had to be brought to the bathrooms by hand and, if a bath was wanted, then many buckets of warm water had to be carried from the kitchen stove to the bedrooms. Meals had to be designed and prepared in discussion with cooks. At least very fresh fish and meat were available in the village. All the vegetables were grown in the large garden and cows were kept for milk and cheese.

Refrigerators did not arrive for most until the late 1950s or early 1960s. From 1909, they were at least lucky to have an icehouse near the garden where perishables could be stored. Ice houses were common on the big estates in the Highlands, around the coast in particular. These were stone-built huts near where ice could be brought ashore from the boats that sometimes found big slabs of winter ice while out fishing. Winter ice was also brought by cart to the ice houses.

I remember the old ice house in the Culag Hotel grounds when I was a child in the 1940s, although no longer in use as refrigerators arrived in the hotel with the installation of an electricity generator by my grandfather in the early 1920s. The Culag ice house had been built in Victorian times by the Duke of Sutherland's family when it was being used as a private hunting and fishing lodge.

Early on, a large laundry had been built to clean and dry clothes, as well as sheets and towels. Drying things in the often wet climate of northern Scotland was always difficult. Fuel for the stoves and boilers came in on the ship, and was also used in the kitchen, as well as, initially, for open fires in each guest room. Central heating was only installed in about 1920. Everything had to be done by hand.

It was fortunate that a lot of the 'props' needed to run a household for the very rich of that time could be brought in by the steamboats that travelled weekly up through the islands off the west coast of Scotland. These goods came straight to the jetty next to the hotel – even some goods not normally available in remote areas could be ordered. A considerable number of staff were needed, far more than the number of guests in the days before electricity and powered machines, and had to be trained by Elsie before being allowed to work closely with the guests.

The other problem, as always in the Highlands, was the midge: minute little insects that attack any bare flesh they can land on. In the 1900s, it was argued that cigarettes were the best protection and many ladies, including my grandmother, tried that. Granny always said it was the midges who got her started – particularly on still days with no wind. She smoked twenty unfiltered Craven As a day until she died at the age of ninety, much to my horror, as a non-smoker. Midges appear to have been designed by nature to keep the tourist hordes from ever wanting to holiday in such locations for too long — when they are busy, one prays for wind!

For Elsie, the ever-changing solutions of the Duke and Duchess of Sutherland in terms of how the hotel would function made for a stressful life. However, she always said she got on very well with Millicent and found her likeable on the fairly frequent occasions when they met and discussed how the hotel was to be run.

Unfortunately, there is still a reluctancy in Sutherland to think well of Millicent, probably because she married into the family associated with the notorious Clearances, but it is worth noting her accomplishments.

Between 1900 and the 1940s, there was only one doctor to look after the sick in the Assynt area and surrounding settlements – Dr Turner, who lived across the bay from the Culag and became a good friend of John's. The nearest hospital in Inverness was over 100 miles away. There was no national health scheme in those days and many could not afford help when ill. To address the problem, Duchess Millicent set up a scheme to train local Highland girls as nurses. She sent the girls at her expense to be trained in London hospitals and then return to work in villages all over Sutherland.

When WWI began, Millicent recruited her own contingent of nurses and took them – again at her own expense – to Belgium and then France to provide nursing cover for the army soldiers. Millicent herself served on the frontline and was nationally recognised for her efforts. After WWI, she stayed in France for a considerable length of time before continuing to make use of the diminishing Sutherland funds towards various schemes to teach skilled trades to northern lads. She also wrote several books.

Elsie's aunt, Jean, was trained under the nursing scheme. After Elsie had five or so miscarriages, Nurse Jean came to stay in the Culag and my mother, Jean, was born with her help. Aunt Jean was also her namesake.

By the time myself and Penny were born, the village had a permanent nurse working with Dr Turner. The daughter of the local nurse from the time that we were babies was still living in the village in 2019 – we met at her Achins Bookshop in Inverkirkaig, near Lochinver.

Nurse Jean and her sister, Christina Mackay

Cars were also much more common which made a big difference to rural health and survival. John bought his first car in 1911 and employed a full-time chauffeur, useful assets for transporting guests. It was only at this time that improvements had begun on road surfaces allowing motorised vehicles access to remote villages. The earlier horse-drawn carriages had made for a bumpy ride. In the time of the Culag Hotel, the roads were initially the responsibility of the landowner but eventually that responsibility was handed over to the County Council.

John's first car (1911)
An Arrol Johnston made in Scotland around 1901

By the 1920s, bus services were also able to make use of the improved roads. Although, by the late 1930s, the roads were much better surfaced, they remained very narrow with passing places to allow cars, lorries, and buses to get to and from Lochinver safely. The passing places still exist on these roads through mountainous areas today, with Lochinver lying on the North Highland Cycle Route – the North Coast 500 – that is very popular with visitors from many countries.

Changing Ownership

The Duke's aim in undertaking the alterations had been to maximise the potential profitability of their building by turning it into a hotel, that should attract affluent visitors. The strategy was, initially, exceptionally successful as the style fitted that of the Edwardian era. When it first opened, during the early 1900s, there were were many people wanting a different type of holiday in a place suitable for an Edwardian gentleman – one who could enjoy the challenge of not just a holiday in the wild landscape but also of making the long and rather adventurous trek to Lochinver.

The wealthy British of the 1900s were, to an extent, mimicking Queen Victoria's obsession with holidaying at Balmoral. Scotland was, then, a fashionable place, so the Duke's idea of a hotel for the wealthy who lacked their own estates was probably a sound business idea – at least, without the intervention of the First World War.

The Duke remained the owner of the hotel until 1913 when he died suddenly just before the war started. His son, the fifth Duke, took over but with the First World War going on, the interest of the Sutherland Estate in the minutiae of running of the hotel disappeared. Likewise, so did the guests – at least for the start of the period. In fact, bookings steadily increased later during WWI as many families who had lost children in the war decided to escape somewhere remote to grieve. The Culag did well financially during WWI.

The land remained under Sutherland family ownership until it had to be sold because of the financial crises around the 1920s and 1930s. Much of the land is now owned by the Duke of Westminster, other parts by the Vestey family who purchased it from the Sutherlands around 1936. The Duke of Westminster bought a substantial part of the Assynt estate inland and to the north, although we believe he also owns some buildings and land in Lochinver. The Vestey family bought much of the west coast Highland estate which had been owned for centuries by the Dukes of Sutherland and their forebears. The Vestey family was one of the richest families in Britain in the 1930s. They had vastly increased their fortune during WWI by bringing food supplies to a beleaguered Britain and continued to thrive even through the financial crises of the 1930s.

On Christmas Day 1929, the Culag suffered a fire – a major event for the Skinner family, mainly remembered by our mother as the Christmas she lost all of her presents! But for her parents, it meant the loss of almost all of their belongings as the furniture and fittings were not fully insured – fortunately, they were able to rescue a few belongings after the fire. The fire engines had to come from Inverness, about 100 miles away along windy roads in winter weather.

The Lodge Hotel

The actual buildings belonged to the owners who, by that time, may have still been the Sutherlands or may have been the Westminsters. The Westminsters were certainly involved in helping to get part of the Skinners' business going again before the Culag was rebuilt.

It would take nine years for the Culag to be rebuilt and once again be usable as a hotel. In the meantime, the Skinners were given run of a small, nine-bedroomed hotel on Lochinver's Main Street known as the Lodge.

Guests returning to the Lodge Hotel after a successful fishing trip

Elsie very quickly got business going in these smaller premises and many of those who came for the excellent fly-fishing and hunting continued to visit annually. John was able to reopen the bar beside the Lochinver jetty to bring in some money while the Culag was rebuilt using the landowner's insurance money.

In 1938, the Culag was ready to reopen after the completion of the work to rebuild on the old foundations. The new Culag Hotel incorporated many of the old features. However, with the tower replaced it was a much smaller hotel. The Skinners paid for the fixtures and the fittings as these were the responsibility of the hotel proprietor.

Elsie, Jean, and John outside the Culag

Setting up the Culag again used up whatever financial resources the Skinners had left. That this event occurred not long before WWII was catastrophic for them – they had no time to recoup their substantial losses. World War II hit them very hard financially, as they relied on visitors coming for holidays. A 1939 government decree had banned anybody who did not have their home in north and west Sutherland from travelling there, fearing enemy landings in that isolated area in the early years of the war. That financial disaster for hotelkeepers just amplified the problems caused in earlier decades by the very difficult national financial situation of the International Bank Crashes of the 1920s and 1930s which had a real impact on just the sort of well-off people who had been their main clientele after WWI. The wartime government decreed nobody who suffered from this regulation could be declared bankrupt – in those days, and for decades afterward, that was considered a social disaster. However, if you had been made bankrupt by using up all your resources to keep the hotel going, which the Skinners had, how could such decrees help?

The Vesteys, being far better businessmen than the Sutherlands, decided to change the way their newly-acquired hotel was run shortly after WWII. Inevitably, this meant bringing in new management. This gave the Skinners no time to rectify the damages done to their finances over the past decade. I remember my grandfather's last visit to the banker, Mr Gordon, in Lochinver, asking him for some sort of financial assistance – I had obviously been taken along to try and soften the banker's heart!

Highland Games in Culag Park. During WWII, this area was
used for grazing milk cows.

The Culag where we grandchildren lived in the 1940s was
a paradise: no shortage of food; lots of safe places to play;
and the land girls who were growing vegetables in the walled
gardens of the hotel and looking after the chickens and milk
cows kept us children amused. There was, of course, the
Lochinver pier where I managed to step off the edge,
fortunately when the tide was out so all I did was fall onto
sand and mud. As Granny could not swim, that really was
lucky! There was also the incident on Achmelvich when I
was rescued from death at the age of three by my mother
who, sitting on the beach with our Campbell cousins, looked
up and saw my floating bottom – just in time to rush in and

pull me out and give me a good, hard shake to get all the water out of me!

My mother, Jean, myself, and my sister, Penny all spent the first years of our lives in Lochinver. I now realise growing up in such a wild and beautiful landscape miles from the nearest town, with people who made their living from the sea and their own small plots of land, had a profound effect on my understanding of the world. The contrast between that and industrial Lancashire to which we moved was the reason I was later to train and practise as a town and environmental planner.

The Culag Hotel in the 1940s – after the rebuild but before the fish processing buildings were constructed

The fully rebuilt Culag Hotel in the 1950s

On a bright sunny day in 1946, we all said goodbye to the Culag and drove across to the east coast of Sutherland. Leaving my first home at the age of five was to prove memorable. Not for any of the right reasons such as sympathy for my grandparents and mother losing what had been their home since 1910 but simply because, as we drove out of Lochinver through woodlands, Elsie suddenly got very excited about seeing a wild cat in the woodland. At the age of five, I was too young to have any real understanding of the events other than my grandparents and mother being very upset.

The Skinners were saved by John's brothers, Donald and Frank, who were also in the hotel-keeping business. Donald had been involved in the herring trade in Wick and then employed as Fisheries Officer in the port of Aberdeen before taking up hotel-keeping. Frank owned hotels in Northern Ireland, Skye, and near Smoo Cave and Overscaig in Lairg in the far northwest.

Frank also owned a small hotel, the Navidale, in the fishing town of Helmsdale. Frank had wanted to open Navidale as a hotel again after it was used as a base for a group from the local RAF squadron towards the end of the war. So he let Elsie and John use the Navidale as a hotel from 1945 while they tried to sort out their financial affairs – thus providing my sister and me with our first post-war home. The Navidale proved to be yet another financial disaster as the strict limit on petrol coupons meant very few visitors until after 1950. Elsie and John ran the Navidale Hotel for three years.

Helmsdale was an equally idyllic place to be as a young child. The air was clean and the food was good and healthy. It was typical crofter's food: vegetables straight from the garden with fresh meat readily available despite the continuation of food rationing and a harbour for fishing boats at the bottom of the hill. I remember my grandfather roasting shellfish for us on a shovel over the fire that he had collected by the harbour.

The Navidale, Helmsdale (1946)

We, as children, met Frank Skinner, our grandfather's half-brother, only fleetingly on several occasions. However, we did grow up knowing our family owed him a debt of gratitude. Why that was, we never really knew as it was never discussed with us children or specified by our grandparents or parents. Now, with all concerned long dead, we can just about surmise what happened.

After our grandmother died, we began to get the true story of what had happened in the 1940s and how Frank bailed John out of an impossible financial mess. All their money had been in the Culag Hotel which, as proprietors, they had to furnish and equip, alongside running it, so that they could pay the rent required by the owners.

I do remember meeting Frank in the 1960s in the room over his shop in Lairg and the enormous glasses of whisky he poured for my mother and father, neither of whom were great drinkers. Unlike Elsie's husband, John, who – having been apprenticed in the brewing and distilling trades before running a hotel – did, indeed, have a taste for a dram.

8. LATER GENERATIONS

Elsie had to move again in the late 1940s as she and her husband, John, had to retire – mostly for financial reasons, although they were both already in their sixties. They gave up running their last hotel – the Navidale, in the small east coast fishing town of Helmsdale – as there were insufficient guests in that time. It was not long after WWII, when petrol rationing was still enforced and so too few visited the far north of Scotland for holidays, making the running of a hotel uneconomic. John's brothers, Donald and Frank Skinner, did their best to help him but there was a sensible limit on the risks they could take to support John financially, as their own hotel businesses and family members suffered at the same time from equal pressures.

For the Skinners, as John was beginning to be not very well by then, it was decided the best solution was to move to live as near as possible to their daughter and three grandchildren, then living in Lancashire, renting somewhere nearby. I do not think when they made that decision that they had any clue about the horrendous conditions in South Lancashire after the war and the lack of decent housing at any time in this industrial area.

No idea, either, about the perpetually filthy air created by the factory chimneys. No idea about the lack of fresh food and how families had to live off post-war food rations; nor about clothing shortages. No idea, really, about what such industrial areas were like and the really poor conditions in which working families had lived before the war, never mind during and after it. In nearby Liverpool, 70,000 were made homeless in the Blitz of 1941.

Britain was economically broke in the late 1940s and it took until the end of the 1960s to return to any level of prosperity in the northern factory towns. The ugliness of their new environment must have depressed them and the only place they could find to rent was a small flat several miles from where the grandchildren lived. They had no means of transport and the trolleybuses were few and far between. We did have a family lunch with them most weekends and my mother often used to take the bus into the town centre to meet them off the bus from their part of the town. However, it cannot have been what they envisaged. John, having smoked a pipe all his life, developed throat cancer and died not long after moving to St Helens. Following this, in 1955, Elsie moved in with us and I remember there was a shuffling round of bedrooms so that she could have a room of her own.

At this time, I was fourteen years old; my sister, twelve; and my brother, eight. The house our father had managed to rent after moving back to live in St Helens when he left the army as a Lieutenant Colonel (Lt Col) was reasonably spacious and, even better, adjoined a large green space – a golf course. It had views of distant hills and, above all, much fresher and less dirty air. The air in St Helens was so dirty that clothes hung out to air-dry came back in dotted with dark splodges, this being in the days before dryers existed. In the housing shortages immediately after the war, one lived anywhere there was an available house and it was not until the late 1950s that we were able to move to healthier places.

I remember we had a network of nearby friends and would frequently play in each other's gardens – we are still in touch with four of them today, more than fifty years later. There was the possibility of playing not just in a substantial garden but, even better, in the adjoining golf course. Provided that we kept to the edges that weren't mown, nobody minded us playing there. Beyond that was Taylor Park, a large Victorian era city park with a very large lake and rowboats for hire. At last, my mother and grandmother got away from the areas of the most polluted, filthy air of the densely-built and, at the time, very smelly industrial towns of Lancashire.

Jean and Elsie in Prescot

Granny's life only became relatively bearable again three years or so after her husband died. At that time, she took over looking after our family home while mother did most of the cooking. I realise now, it must have been for her a bit like being back in the croft where she spent so much of her time on housework and rearing children.

Elsie at ninety years old with the Mayor

Elsie settled down in this house but then we moved to the next house which had much more room so as to be nearer good schools. It, too, had a large garden which she enjoyed and was very near expansive green spaces so the air was cleaner. The major green space we used at this time was Knowsley Park – a grand estate with extensive grounds. As our father was known to the owner, Lord Derby, from his army days, our family were able to walk the private parkland almost whenever we wanted – at least until the late 1960s, when it became a Wild Animal Safari Park, which one had to pay to enter.

Not long after that, in 1971, Elsie died at the age of ninety-one. She remained very fit all of her life, most likely due to being someone who was active every day and had been from childhood working on her parents' croft. That, and keeping her mind active by reading books and doing the crossword every day until her last year, by which time she was at least living in a less polluted area of Lancashire.

Our parents then moved to Formby on the Lancashire Coast to be near the sea as we children had all left home by then. That was a much more liveable environment for our mother, allowing daily seaside walks, at least for a few years before she became unable to walk. Unfortunately, she then developed leukaemia and died some years later after a very long fight during which she put herself on a very strict diet which did keep her going far longer than doctors expected at the time for someone in her condition. Our father moved to another house in Formby and was lucky enough to persuade a lovely friend to marry him. He died in 2000 but our delightful stepmother, Jean Rollo, stayed on and we visit fairly often. Jean is also descended from Scottish relatives, some of whom were founding members of the Scottish National Party (SNP).

Elsie was always so proud of what her siblings did with their lives. They remained close, despite the physical distance between them. We most often met Elsie's siblings on their visits to Lairg, where they would get together in Hector Mackay's home, Sydney House, after Torroble croft became virtually abandoned. Elsie got on very well with Hector's housekeeper, Mrs Elphinstone. I got the impression, in the 1950s and 1960s, that Elsie really liked talking to her so she could find out about her old friends from Lairg, as well as those from her Lochinver days.

In retrospect, I realise now – being old myself – just how lonely Granny must have felt from the 1950s onwards. She had a very dull life living with us in Lancashire, I am afraid – nobody to talk with who knew anything about her life before, being classed by people as just another old dame. I do remember Granny and my mother discussing fairly scandalous tales about the local well-off of Sutherland and others that Mrs Elphinstone had told them but I confess now I cannot even remember the names of the people involved. However, Mrs Elphinstone did work for James Robertson

Justice, the fairly notorious actor, in his little 'castle' holiday home for quite some time. In any case, those visits and the talks she had there really did entertain Granny and cheer her up.

Elsie was always very proud of what her brothers and sisters had achieved with their lives and enjoyed talking about them all but sadly, half of her siblings had left Lairg for Canada, the USA, or New Zealand and she inevitably saw little of them. After the war years, Granny's brothers and sisters, as well as other family members, visited from time to time from across the world. Following her death, they continued to visit our mother, until they, too, became too elderly. They frequently stayed with our family on these visits, as well as with Kate in Northumberland and Donald's daughter, Elizabeth, in Devon.

We knew her sisters, Kate and Hannah, best and the sibling Elsie saw most throughout her life was Kate. In April 1961, my parents took Kate, then in her seventies, and Elsie, in her eighties, as well as my brother on an overland trip to Italy, including Rome, Florence, and Venice, a trip which seemed to please both women very much.

Kate was another very hardworking woman, following the example of their own hardworking mother in Torroble. She, characteristically, was a very good manager and organiser and I remember her as a no-nonsense woman, one who I admit likely thought me a lazy and hopeless great-niece as all I did was sit and read – not how a Mackay should behave!

Jean, Ian, Kate, and Elsie in Florence (1961)

Kate was very kind and every year, often over the Easter holiday, had us children to stay at Dunstanburgh Castle Hotel, in Embleton near the sea, for a week at at time. As Hannah did not live far away in Ashington, we would usually see her at the same time. I remember her homemade ginger wine particularly well. You could tell she had been a school teacher from the way she looked at you.

Elsie was totally grief-stricken when Kate died as she had looked after her as a baby on the croft in Torroble and had always taken a close interest in her life, particularly as Kate was also in the hotel-keeping business.

I remember once waving Elsie's brother, Alec, and his wife, Helen, off in Liverpool Docks when they left for the US after staying with us. It was a memorable encounter as our mother developed pneumonia very soon afterwards and we always blamed that on the visit Father took Alec, Helen, and Mother on to north Wales – perhaps to convince them that living in the then filthy dirty air of industrial Lancashire was not really so bad! I also visited Helen in the USA in the 1980s.

We saw little of John and his wife, Annie, although we did stay a night with them in Lairg in the mid 1950s. The siblings I never met were: Julia, who lived in Edinburgh; Jean, who lived in New Zealand; Robert, who died young in the Bronx; and James, who died before WWI. We only met Donald once, when we were too young to remember, although we are now very pleased to be in contact with his daughter, Elizabeth, having previously met once around 1946.

Bill, and his granddaughter, Donna, from New Zealand visited Elizabeth in Devon when he was on his tours of Britain, undertaken so he could write his most useful booklet of the Family Tree of the Acheilidh Mackays of Sutherland,

Scotland, which he distributed to every relative in New Zealand and elsewhere. Elizabeth says her greatest thrill was to visit Bill and Belle in Gore in 1991 when she and her husband, Colin, spent nearly three months in New Zealand. They met up with many of the New Zealand relatives and still keep in touch, at least at Christmastime. My sister, Penny, also made visits to family members in New Zealand.

Bill and Belle

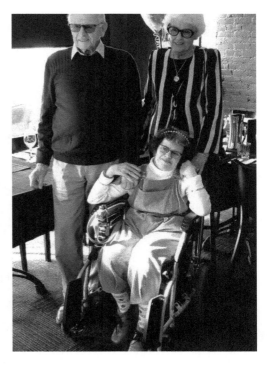

Ted, Dorothy, and Nicky

I visited Donna twice in Melbourne. Once was after my first visit to Perth as a judge on the Perth foreshore redesign competition when I was able to take the time to travel. The second occasion, several years later, was after she had moved house, but was still in Melbourne. Her children were then still in their early teens. Prior to that, I had several times driven Donna around in England when she was here visiting relatives. The last time I saw her in England was in the 1970s when I took her from my parents' home in Lancashire to stay with Kate in her hotel in Northumberland.

Elizabeth is in touch as part of this project to provide information about the Torroble family and, in particular, about Donald's and her own lives for these family stories. Growing up in Lairg, Elizabeth remembers meeting several Mackay cousins, including Hector of Sydney House, as well as Hector Ross, Tina Campbell, and Mary Davidson.

All through the war years and the decades after until her death, we were in regular touch with Julia's daughter, Meg Campbell. Our mother, Meg's cousin, together with our father, went to see Meg after Jimmy died and she returned to the Highlands from a married life mainly spent near London. She had a lovely cottage overlooking the sea in Plockton, one of the north's most charming villages and my father would visit her there.

We've had no luck locating her children. I did try, so as to verify parts of this part of family story. Helen, Alec's wife, had a visit from Fiona once and thought she had trained as an accountant and married a MacBain – someone involved in finance and the oil industry, living in Aberdeen. Unfortunately, we had no further luck in tracking her down. Later, someone said Fiona might have died but I could not find evidence of her online either way.

Plockton

Meg's other daughter, Catherine, was a good artist and was supposedly working as an illustrator for books produced by the AA Roads in the 1960s and 1970s. Their son, Colin, we remember as being interested in Geology and panning for gold when he was young.

I believe this information may have come via my mother or father from Hannah's son, Cyril Bainbridge, at one of their last meetings. They visited our family in Lancashire quite a few times in the 1950s and Granny and Ma really enjoyed those visits – they were both so nice to us as children and we looked forward to their visits. Chris, in particular, was kind to us.

It is such a pity we never had proper contact when younger but Granny never wanted to bother people and my mother was a bit the same.

The Enduring Mackay Line

Elizabeth Healy

Christina Mackay (1922-2014), known as Chris, was the first child of young Donald and Elizabeth Mackay (known as Lizzie). Chris was born at Lower Torroble on 29th June 1922. She attended Lairg School and then went to work for Hector

Ross at the Sutherland Arms Hotel, Dornoch. She was called up to serve in the Auxiliary Territorial Service (ATS), deployed to Austria, where she met her future husband Robert (Bob) Henderson (1920-1999). On leaving the services she worked in a bank in Edinburgh until her marriage in July 1948. The newly married couple lived in Edinburgh for some time before setting up in their own home in East Lothian where their two daughters were born. They stayed in the same home until their deaths in 1999. Chris had two granddaughters.

Elizabeth, Alistair, Chris, Hamish, and Jenny at a family wedding (1989)

Janet MacEwan Mackay (1925-2001), known as Jenny, was the second born child. She was born at Lower Torroble on 18th January 1925. She attended Lairg School and then went to work as a domestic for a Kate Mackay – a first cousin of her grandfather, Donald. She was called up to serve with the Women's Royal Air Force (WRAF) but only served in the UK. She met her husband to be George Smith (1923-2012) during this time and they were married on 16th November 1946 in Leicester. They had one daughter and lived in Leicester all their married lives. Jenny had two grandsons.

James Donald Mackay (1929-2014), known as Hamish, was the first son of Donald and Elizabeth. He was born at Gower House, Main Street, Lairg on 30th January 1929. His early schooling must have been spent at a local school to the Gordonbush Estate, near Brora, but later he attended Lairg School, as well as joining a local cadet force. Upon leaving school, he joined the local Post Office as a telegram boy. He progressed to be fully employed in the Post Office – a very busy office at this time as passenger mail buses travelled daily to the north and west of Sutherland, delivering all mail plus goods. Following National Service with the Royal Signals 1946-47, he returned to the local Post Office before going on to work for the Post Office in Rhodesia. Returning home in around 1954/55 he continued working at the Lairg Post Office until retirement, achieving the grade of Postmaster.

He married his wife Helen (1930-2020) in October 1956 and they lived in Lairg until their respective deaths, having raised two daughters and a son. Like his father, Hamish was a keen fisherman and in retirement acted as a gillie for clients on the River Oykell. Hamish had three grandsons.

Alexander MacEwan Mackay (b. 1930), known as Alastair, was the second son. He was born on 13th December 1930 at Gordonbush, near Brora. After the family moved back to Lairg, he attended Lairg school, being picked up each morning with his brother by a special school bus that collected children from outlying areas. The family moved to live on the Lochside area of the village in late 1940. Having completed his years at school, Alastair went to work at Lairg Lodge. He joined the Royal Air Force (RAF) in 1948 and served for eight years, both at home and abroad.

Upon returning home, he got a job with Wimpey as an onsite electrician during the building of the Dam on Loch Shin. On completion of the building work in 1958 he was employed by the North of Scotland Hydro Electric Board, where he was the first employee of the Shin scheme at Cassley Power Station. In 1971 he moved with his family to Rannoch from where he progressed to Senior Control Engineer until his retirement in 1993. He married his first wife in 1960 and they had four children in the next six years, three sons and a daughter.

They divorced in 1976 and Alistair married his present wife Edna in 1979. They both continue to live in Perthshire. Alistair has six granddaughters and one grandson.

Elizabeth Mackay (b. 1940), the third daughter, was born on 28th August 1940 at Gruids, Lairg, where the family found temporary accommodation on return from Gordonbush. The young baby Elizabeth spent much of her childhood unaware of what her older sisters were doing in their lives. Any rivalry between her and her brothers later turned into very strong bonds between all of the family.

She attended Lairg school but her secondary education was spent as a boarder at Dornoch Academy as Lairg school had been downgraded by the early 1950s. She went on to nursing in Edinburgh, where she spent any spare time visiting her sister Chris and family. Her love of children led her to take up employment with a well-known family in Perthshire as a nanny to two small children. The family also had an estate in Sutherland and so several months in the summer were spent there.

Elizabeth married Colin in March 1963 and moved to live in Devon. Her husband was a serviceman, and although they moved several times in the early years, including two years in Canada, Exmouth became their favourite home. They have four sons, four granddaughters, and three grandsons.

In summary, Donald Mackay (son of Donald Mackay of Torroble) and Elizabeth (née Dunn) had three daughters and two sons, six granddaughters and eight grandsons. There are now a total of fourteen great-granddaughters and nine great-grandsons plus two great-great grandsons.

The Beers

My father, Geoffrey Beer, was a Londoner by birth who went to St Paul's School in London before working for the Ordnance Survey. He then joined a management trainee course at Pilkington Brothers glass manufacturers just before the war. At that time, he joined the territorial army so that, in 1939, he was with the regiment that was sent from St Helens to Orkney.

He met our mother in Orkney when his TA regiment of Anti-Aircraft Gunners was posted there on the first day of the war in 1939 to defend the fleet at Scapa Flow or perhaps because some ignoramus in the War Ministry thought Lancashire was near Orkney – both, in their minds, being in the far north!

Jean, as with all unmarried young women in the country then, had to register as being available for war service. She did so on day one, registering where she lived in Inverness.

She was sent after a week's training in Inverness, to Orkney for no better reason than that she could type and the Gunners' officers needed a secretary. As luck would have it both our father and mother were allocated the same digs with a Mr and Mrs Towers – with whom they kept in touch for years after the war and who we children met fairly often.

Jean

Elsie with Jean and Helena just before they reported for duty to their regiments (Jean to Orkney, Helena to Kenya)

Geoffrey Beer (1913-2000)

By then being a Major, Father could not, under army regulations, marry her, a Private soldier. At the beginning of WWII, there was a need to supplement the number of women officers in the Auxiliary Territorial Service (ATS) – the women's branch of the army. So, he solved the marriage problem by sending her to Officer Training in the ATS unit based in Durham which was looking to recruit "well-educated young ladies". This, she definitely was.

After finishing school, Jean was awarded a scholarship to Oxford in 1936 – the only person in the north of Scotland to be awarded one that year. Unfortunately, the scholarship only covered teaching and not living expenses. Her parents, who were struggling financially at the time, could not risk covering her living expenses so she turned the scholarship down. Her old school friends from the Heatherley Boarding School in Inverness were pleased by this decision, so that she should not risk becoming a 'blue stocking' (an intellectual or literary woman) – the greatest of insults in those days as far as young women were concerned!

Instead, she spent a year at the Hotel School in Lausanne, Switzerland after which she spent time working in the Station Hotel, Inverness as work experience. She later went on to study German at Liverpool University. Jean was a superb linguist, as is my brother, Ian, who took after her. Both learned to speak many languages.

Jean and Geoffrey's wedding in Inverness (1941)

A year after Jean was sent to Officer Training, she and Father married and, a year after that, I arrived in Lochinver; my sister, Penelope, just over a year later.

We were incredibly lucky to be brought up as young children in such a beautiful and safe environment, far from any war. We were largely brought up by our grandparents and mother while living in the Culag Hotel in Lochinver, having the run of its corridors and grounds. Meanwhile, our father, having been moved from Orkney to London with his gunners, was in the thick of the Battle of Britain, working in the control center for RAF flights and directing the use of anti-aircraft guns in London.

Geoffrey Beer (left) with the Commanding Officer and others in a London bunker during the Battle of Britain (1940)

He served in the Forces for all six years of the war and finished it as a Lieutenant Colonel. After the war, one had to take whatever job was offered. In Father's case, he was lucky to be offered his old job back in the personnel department of Pilkington Brothers.

At this time, we were still living in at the Navidale Hotel in Helmsdale with our grandparents. We remained there while Father returned to St Helens, first to reclaim the car he had left in storage all through the war in a garage owned by his firm which was, amazingly, still in working order.

Me, my mother, and Penny on Culag Loch (1944)

Father remained at Pilkington Brothers until he retired. It was a time of job shortages and the rationing of foodstuffs and clothes, as well as fuel. These fuel shortages made travel difficult. At that time, people moved wherever jobs and housing were available. In many of the bombed areas of Britain, there was a great shortage of housing.

With Father's job in a very industrial part of Lancashire, that was where we ultimately moved to in 1948. Elsie and her husband, who was not very well, moved there too, so Mother could help look after them. Father only found our first family house in England in 1947 thanks to the help of the wartime army network, the same year that our brother, Ian, was born. It happened that the medic with his regiment in 1939, Dr Edwards, was going home to open his own medical surgery in Widnes and was able to tell him about a vacant house in Widnes next door to him.

When we arrived in Widnes, I was six years old, Penny was four, and my mother was pregnant with Ian. To us, used to living in large hotels run by our grandparents, the house seemed very small.

I had been attending school in Helmsdale for over a year before we moved south into England so, once settled in Widnes, I was sent to the nearby council school which I did not enjoy. Gradually, things appeared to be settling down, despite the very different living conditions in such an industrial town.

Elsie was the kindest of grandmothers and I, a stroppy teenager when living in St Helens with her, was far from a kind child to an old lady. The only nice thing I did – that I fear was motivated by my self interest at that age – was to do the weekly trip to St Helens Library to get books for both of us to read. For me, that had the advantage that I could take more books out than normally allowed and take out 'proper' books not just children's books. I was a voracious reader – it was that which began my self education, from which I learned more than any schooling.

My mother was so concerned that I spent all my time reading that, one day, she summoned the local doctor – at that time, doctors still came to the house when people were ill. He, an army friend of my father's, told her not to be silly. In my mother's mind, the problem was all tied up with the fact I was doing very badly at school.

Like my mother, I too missed the Highlands as I had lived there beside the sea until I was seven years old. I did really very badly at all of the first four schools I went to before I was eleven years old. My mother, who had been a brilliant child, could not figure me out. In Helmsdale school in 1947, a female teacher, who had taught her in the 1920s and also taught me when I was five years old, took her aside and said,

"Jean, I am afraid Anne is just plain stupid." I had obviously not impressed her. I remember her well though, as the Helmsdale school in 1947 was in an old, chapel-like building where the children sat on tiered benches in a semicircle and were taught to write using a slate with a hard pointed chalk-like stone to form the letters and a wet cloth to clear the surface. As for numbers, I was hopeless. For a mother who herself had been brilliant, this was far from good news.

These days I know I am dyslexic which made school an almost catastrophic experience. In the 1950s the word did not exist, nor the comprehension that it often goes with dyspraxia, and clumsy I always was, a characteristic that also inhibited making friends easily when I was very young – who wants to have a clumsy playmate?

It was not until secondary school that I began to understand what I needed to do and, at that stage, found that through the masses of books I had read I had somehow taught myself a great deal. I had, in fact, taught myself to read despite dyslexia and, in my early teens, I used to read by torchlight in bed much to my father's disapproval. I remained bad at writing and, to this day, spelling is highly variable!

My wide reading meant I knew far more about history, geography, society, and economics than most of the other girls in my class and happily answered questions even if I could not write down what needed saying without making mistakes. That I still could not write well and spelled atrociously remained a hindrance but I overcame that with the aid of a couple of brilliant teachers – thank you, Blodwen Lewis of Ruthin and Miss Fitzhenry of somewhere in the south, both outstanding teachers and incredibly kind to a lost child at Huyton College in the 1950s. Their help, together with my accidental discovery that one could add maps and diagrams to essays and be praised for showing such initiative, now makes me smile.

By the time I was sixteen years old, I had found my way through most of these disadvantages and even found ways of making proper long-term friends. By eighteen years old, I was doing Geography at university, finding that map and diagram drawing actually pleased geographers and that seminar groups relied on talking not writing. As such, I survived and then went on to study Civic Design where, again, my drawing abilities proved useful.

Upon my retirement, I moved with my partner, Meta van der Knaap, to the countryside of south Cumbria to enjoy fresh air, lots of green, lakes and rivers, and, once more in my life, be surrounded by hills. With a large garden to make here she, a Dutch landscape designer, created something very special and, even better, she put up with me for over forty years before dying in 2013. The garden still flourishes now, enjoyed by my brother, Ian, myself, and, sometimes, my sister, Penny who is moving back to live in Cumbria, too.

Penny worked for various big organisations including for the US Army in Germany and as a medical secretary for the World Health Organisation (WHO) in Geneva. She then set up her own business as a therapist. Ian studied Philosophy, Politics, and Economics at Oxford and International Relations at the London School of Economics before training as an accountant. He specialised in Local Authority financial matters to make a living. However, his real interest in life is languages – he even has a little Gaelic!

Penny in Acheilidh (2019)

Ian and me in Acheilidh (2019)

9. CLOSING NOTES

In writing this history, I was astonished to realise how far back my own direct link to family history stretched, just through our grandmother telling us her family stories as children – stories which were relayed to her initially by her own parents and grandparents, who themselves had known and been told family stories by their grandparents. This tradition of oral storytelling left me with a family history going back to the 1780s – just through my grandmother with whom I lived for over thirty years.

From Granny's stories about the many ups and downs of life on a croft and how the women coped when the men were away during WWI, we learned what life threw at people and how her siblings coped living in other countries once they left Torroble.

I am the great-great-great grandchild of the crofters who were allocated land by the Duchess of Sutherland's factors from 1812 onwards when the Torroble land was one of the four New Model Farms that the Sutherland Estate created in Lairg. These Model Farms were laid out on old crofting land not long after the first major phases of the Highland Clearances in the Lairg area. That first phase of the Clearances saw many thousands brutally thrown off the land from which they supported family life for centuries, all done by the Sutherland estate factors partly with the aid of some soldiers. It was an event replicated elsewhere in the far north and west of Scotland. There is no definite record as to how many were moved during the Clearances but research suggests it must have been in the tens of thousands, at least. Many left for Canada, the USA, Australia, and New Zealand.

The Mackays were a local clan and loyal to the Earls of Sutherland for centuries, obliged to fight for the Sutherlands whenever requested in return for plots of land supposedly sufficient to support family life. Not something easy at any time in an area of exceptionally poor quality farm land, due to local geology and the cool climate. These days the main industry is tourism and Lairg's many old crofts now operate as bed and breakfasts – neat little houses first built in the mid 1800s to provide a home for each crofting family.

Elsie was left with a passionate understanding of periods of Scottish history. In particular, her retellings of her great-uncle, Alexander's, tales ensured Elsie was vitriolic about what had happened during the time of the Clearances. This normally quiet woman was still angry about what had happened to her people almost a century earlier. She ensured we, her grandchildren born in the 1940s, knew what had happened and how cruelly families were treated. As a child, I always thought she was talking about ancient history but, in writing these stories, I have come to realise she would have known families whose immediate relatives were directly affected by events. What happened to her own immediate forebears was very different, as they were among the relatively few able to stay on or very near the same land their families held crofts on for many years.

The stories here span the period from 1850 to 2020 and are about how one family was lucky enough to overcome the impact of their place and time in history by not just surviving but, for the most part, thriving in life in later decades. This ability to thrive applied not just to those members of the family who stayed in Scotland but to those who emigrated, too.

Until her last weeks, Elsie could be found pottering around in the garden, tidying up the plants, as well as tidying her room upstairs – something she insisted on doing even as she neared her ninetieth year. She read voraciously, sending me off to pick up books for her, first from the St. Helens Library and then the Prescot Library. Whether Elsie actually liked my choices of reading for her, I these days doubt but I cannot remember her complaining.

Elsie ensured we would know of her family history and that we three grandchildren, who lived with her all our childhood, would learn from both grandparents We grew up feeling very much half Scottish and half English as our father was born at the opposite end of Britain, in London.

In unearthing Elsie's life story, it has surprised me just how much she did, probably deliberately, to ensure a good life not just for her daughter, Jean, but also her granddaughters, myself and Penelope, who spent much of our childhood years living with her.

Descendants of the children of Torroble are now spread throughout the world. Over the past one hundred years, many have visited, particularly from New Zealand and Australia. Some twenty years ago, it was calculated there were about 150 direct relatives of Elspeth's and their own children and grandchildren living in New Zealand. By now, we can only surmise that there are many more cousins but my part of the family have lost touch, as my mother's generation of contacts died out with her in 1981.

As we, the Beer family, understand it, there is a younger generation of children in New Zealand or Australia, and maybe even American descendants of the Rogart branch of the Mackay family brought up in Acheilidh croft. There appear to be descendants, too, in Nova Scotia, Canada. In Britain, the bloodline continues with Elizabeth's grandchildren.

Descendants of the Mackays in New Zealand (1966)

Top: Bill Mackay, James Richard Roche, Ross Anthony Ransom,
Frederick P.A.J. Ransom, Edward George Smith

Middle: Cheryl Vivienne Roche, Donna Marie Roche, Isabella Mackay,
Dorothy Matilda Mackay, Mildred Isabelle Mackay, Gayelyn Ann Roche,
Chrissie Jean Mackay, Heather Lorraine Ransom

Bottom: Richard William Roche, Deborah Kaye Roche, James Maurice
Roche, Nicola Anne Smith, Karen Mary Roche, Janine Gay Roche

Appendices and Bibliography

<u>Appendix A:</u> Maps of the Region – Margaret Crane

1. Orkney
2. Lewis
3. Wick
4. Lochinver
5. Loch Assynt
6. Brora
7. Lairg
8. Rogart
9. Ullapool
10. Dornoch

11. Skibo
12. Inverness
13. Perth
14. Edinburgh
15. Glasgow

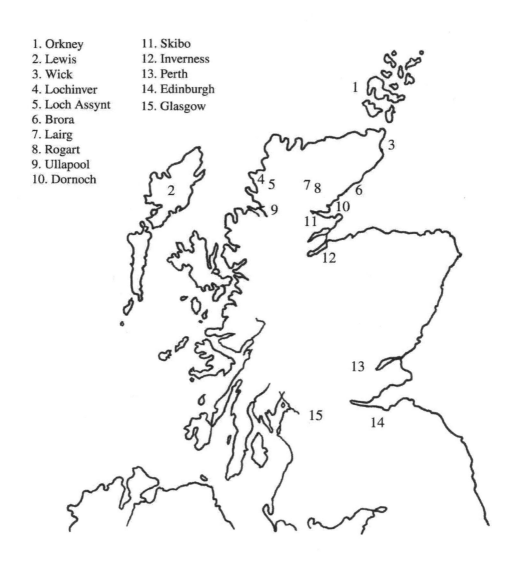

Edinburgh to London - 402 Miles

Location of Family Crofts in Lairg and Rogart

1. Little Loch Shin
2. Lairg School
3. Lairg Station
4. Torroble

5. Balloan
6. Sydney House
7. Dola
8. Loch Craggie

9. Tomich
10. Kinvonvie
11. Acheilidh
12. Rogart Church

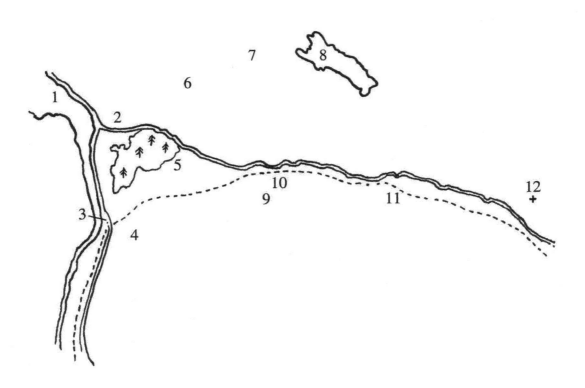

- - - Railway Line

Lairg to Acheilidh 5.8 miles. Acheilidh to Rogart 5.4 miles.

Appendix B: Earlier Generations of The Torroble Mackays[13]

Children of each couple are indicated by italics.

Elspet Murray	Mary MacLeod
(1770-1858)	(b.1776)
Angus Matheson	Hugh Sutherland
(b.1770)	(b.1775)
Jane Matheson	*Christina Sutherland*
(1800-1882)	*(1795-1875)*
Sylvia Lidbetter	Margaret Sutherland
(1760-1830)	(1759-1841)
Iain Matheson	Donald Mackay
(1760-1820)	(1755-1841)
Alexander Matheson	*John Mackay*
(1784-1851)	*(1794-1857)*
Jane Matheson	Christina Sutherland
Alexander Matheson	John Mackay
Johanna Mackay	*John Mackay*
(1824-1902)	*(1820-1902)*

Johanna Mackay
John Mackay
Christina Mackay
(1854-1920)

---

[13] The accuracy of names and dates of earlier generations is to the best of our knowledge.

Gilles MacLeod
(d.1840)
Angus Gunn
(1755-1830)
Elspet Gunn
(1788-1876)

Jean Mackay
John Grant
(1730-1814)
Donald Grant
(1787-1813)

Elspet Gunn
Donald Grant
Julia Grant
(1819-1880)

Elspet Gunn
(b.1741)
William MacLeod
(b.1740?)
Jane Mackay
(1780-1851)

Lille Macpherson
(b.1749)
William Mackay
(b.1750)
James Mackay
(1773-1851)

Jane MacLeod
James Mackay
Hector Mackay
(1815-1899)

Julia Mackay
Hector Mackay
Donald Mackay
(1849-1932)

<u>Appendix C:</u> Linking the Acheilidh and Torroble Mackays -

Christina Mackay

John Mackay (1774-1857) m Christina Sutherland (1797-1875) Acheilidh, Sutherland, SCOTLAND

John Mackay (1820-1902) m Johanna Matheson (1824-1902) Balone, Sutherland, SCOTLAND	Donald Mackay (1822-1888) m Henrietta Matheson (1832-1886) Lairg, Sutherland, SCOTLAND	Mary Ann Mackay (1826-1918) m James Todd (1829-1891) Geelong, Victoria, AUSTRALIA	Hugh Mackay (1828-1875) – Acheilidh, Sutherland, SCOTLAND	James Mackay (1830-1904) m Jane Gillanders (1830-1916) Longbush, Southland, NZ	Angus W Mackay (1834-1917) m Isabella Helm (1841-1873) Longbush, Southland, NZ	Mur (18 m A (18 A Su SC

John Mackay (1847 -1927) m Jane McKinna (1860-1948) Otama, Southland, NZ	Alexander Mackay (1851-1902) m Alice Stott (1862-1893) Riversdale, Southland, NZ	Christina Mackay (1853-1920) m Donald Mackay (1849-1932) Torroble, Sutherland, SCOTLAND	Jean Mackay (b.1855) m James Sutherland m Angus Mackay Sutherland, SCOTLAND	William Mackay (1858-1915) m Georgina McKenzie (1864-1939) Riversdale, Southland, NZ	Donald Mackay (1863-1912) m Elizabeth McGillivray (1866-1951) Lairg, Sutherland, SCOTLAND	C I (18

Elspeth Mackay (1880-1971) m John Skinner

...Mackay (...1893) (Lena) ...nro (...1919) ...ilidh, ...rland, ...LAND	Alexander Mackay (1839-1918) — Acheilidh, Sutherland, SCOTLAND					

| ...stina ...kay (...1876) — — | John Mackay (b.1877) m Christina Leslie (1892-1974) — | Angus Mackay (1878-1941) — — | Christina Mackay (1880-1946) — — | Marion Mackay (1881-1934) m Duncan Campbell (1857-1934) — | Dolina Mackay (b.1885) m James Matheson (b.1886) — | William Mackay (1887-1975) m Ruth Munro (1901-1983) Acheilidh, Sutherland, SCOTLAND |

James Murdo Mackay (1931-2021)

m. Anne Corbett

Acheilidh, Sutherland, SCOTLAND

Appendix D: The Development of Textiles in the U.K. - Jane Mallinson

Until the late 1700s the majority of people wore wool or linen, these being homegrown products processed locally where they were produced. For richer people, cotton came from India and silks from China, and were processed where they were grown.

The industrial revolution began with various inventions beginning most importantly with James Watt's steam engine which enabled cloth production to be mechanised. Hargreaves' spinning jenny and Crompton's mule meant fine spun cotton could be mass-produced. This was followed by Cartwright's power loom to weave the spun yarn. The damp atmosphere of the west of the U.K. was conducive to cotton spinning, cotton being of such a short staple, the damp helped it to stick together.

This coincided with a vast increase in cotton plantations in America and the invention of Eli Whitney's cotton gin which removed the seeds from the cotton boll.

The port of Glasgow meant that Scottish processing of American cotton developed locally. The philanthropist Robert Owen famously built cotton mills at New Lanark providing better working conditions, good houses for his workers, and education for children.

The bobbin industry of the Lake District powered by water wheels, developed to supply the growing number of mills with the thousands of bobbins needed for spun yarn.

Within 50 years, the cottage industry producing woollen cloth made from local sheep all but collapsed, but a few weavers like Silas Marner remained.

Appendix E: The Torroble Siblings

Julia Mackay (1875-1939) m. John Campbell
Margaret Campbell

Hannah Mackay (1878-1956) m. Ernest Bainbridge
Cyril Bainbridge

Elspeth Mackay (1880-1971) m. John Skinner
Jean Skinner (1917-1981)

Jean Mackay (1882-1942) m. Innaeas Mackay
Chrissie Mackay (1922-2008)

Hector Mackay (1883-1887)

John Mackay (1885-1956) m. Annie Murray

Hector Mackay (1887-1954) m. Lavinia Cumming (1885-1960)

Alexander Mackay (1889-1975) m. Helen Daniels

Robert Mackay (1892-1945) m. Katherine Grieve

James Mackay (1894-1914)

Donald Mackay (1895-1968) m. Elizabeth Hepburn Dunn
(1898-1972)
Christina Mackay (1922-1999)
Janet Mackay (1925-2001)
James Mackay (1929-2014)
Alexander Mackay (b.1930)
Elizabeth Mackay (b.1940)

Catherine Mackay (1897-1965) m. Tommy Robson
Alistair Robson

William Mackay (1899-1994) m. Isabella
Mildred Mackay
Dorothy Mackay

Bibliography

Cunningham, Tom (2008) *Your Fathers the Ghosts: Buffalo Bill's Wild West in Scotland.* Black and White Publishing.

Ketteringham, Lesley (2004) *A History of Lairg.* Lairg Local History Society.

Macdonald, John (2002) *Rogart: The Story of a Sutherland Crofting Parish.* Rogart Heritage Society.

McPherson, Flora (1993) *Watchman Against the World – The Remarkable Journey of Norman McLeod.* Breton Books.

Pennant, Thomas (1769) *A Tour in Scotland.*

Privel, Marlyn (Ed.) (2018) A History of Settlement in Lairg. Lairg Local History Society.

Uncles, Christopher J. (2007) *Memories of East Sutherland.* Stenlake Publishing.

Uncles, Christopher J. (2003) *Memories of North and West Sutherland.* Stenlake Publishing.

List of Images

All images are from the author's family archives unless otherwise stated.

A Brief History of Sutherland

The Acheilidh Mackays

The Torroble Siblings

Lochinver

The Culag Years (1910-1946)

Later Generations

Closing Notes

Cathel MacLeod

Lochinver, Sutherland

cmacleod331@gmail.com

About the Author

Anne R. Beer is a retired environmental planner, and Professor Emeritus in the Department of Landscape at the University of Sheffield. She can be contacted at anne.beer41@me.com.

Suzey Ingold is a freelance editor and writer of fiction and non-fiction, currently based in Toronto, Canada. She can be contacted via her website, suzeysays.com.